Shimmers of Light

Shimmers of Light

Spiritual Reflections for the Christmas Season

CHUCK QUEEN

RESOURCE *Publications* · Eugene, Oregon

SHIMMERS OF LIGHT
Spiritual Reflections for the Christmas Season

Copyright © 2011 Chuck Queen. All rights reserved. Except for brief quotations in critical publications or reviews, no part of this book may be reproduced in any manner without prior written permission from the publisher. Write: Permissions, Wipf and Stock Publishers, 199 W. 8th Ave., Suite 3, Eugene, OR 97401.

Resource Publications
An Imprint of Wipf and Stock Publishers
199 W. 8th Ave., Suite 3
Eugene, OR 97401
www.wipfandstock.com

ISBN 13: 978-1- 61097-002-0

Manufactured in the U.S.A.

All Scripture quotations, unless otherwise indicated, are taken from the New Revised Standard Version Bible, copyright 1989, by the Division of Christian Education of the National Council of the Churches of Christ in the U.S.A, and are used by permission. All rights reserved.

*To my granddaughter,
Sophie Jordyn Griffith, born June 17, 2010.
After I have departed this world,
my hope is that she will still find something
of value in these pages.*

Contents

Introduction ix

1 Everyday Thankfulness 1
    Shimmers of Gratitude

2 Advent's Invitation 13
    Shimmers of Hope

3 Awakenings 25
    Shimmers of Renewal

4 The Way of Peace 39
    Shimmers of a World Made Whole

5 The Heart of the Universe 58
    Shimmers of Divine Love

6 The Love that Sent Him 73
    Shimmers of Transforming Grace

7 God With Us 88
    Shimmers of a Deeper Joy

Bibliography 103

Introduction

ONE YEAR during the Christmas season an article appeared in a local paper titled, "Frenzy over Furby fuels beginning of Christmas shopping season." The Furby, many will remember, was a cute, fluffy thing with pointed ears that looked like a Gremlin. Remember the movie *Gremlins* and what happened when a Gremlin got wet? It underwent a transformation of character and appearance, and was no longer cute and cuddly. The article in the paper pointed out that the shoppers lined up outside of Wal–Mart on Black Friday, looked like Gremlins that had gotten a good soaking.

Some shoppers had been waiting all night and were first in line. As it neared six o'clock in the morning, when the doors would open, the crowd outside swelled and a few late arrivals slipped in toward the front. That's when the mood turned ugly. Police officers were called in. One officer announced through a loud speaker, over the nasty clamor and ill will of shoppers, "Everyone's an adult here. Don't cut line. This is a bad way to start the Christmas season." In the end, even threats of handcuffs and police custody couldn't keep shoppers from sprinting into the store as workers swung the doors open. Some shoppers were almost trampled in the wild scramble to get to the Furbys first. Other shoppers, however, didn't seem to mind. One woman said, "It's exhilarating; it's like a rush."

I suppose that for some folks this is what Christmas is mainly about. I am reminded of two sisters who expressed mild irritation while looking at a Christmas display. That year, the store decided not to display its traditional Santa Clause with Santa's elves and reindeer. Instead, it featured a church with lovely carols ringing out, an enormous star shining brilliantly above, and a cloud of angels faintly glowing in the dark sky. One sister turned to the other and said, "Stella, look at that! If we don't watch out the church is going to take over Christmas!" Imagine that—the church taking over Christmas.

Christmas has come to involve twenty-four hour shopping opportunities, with music blaring, lights blinking, and an unceasing dispensing of holiday cheer. There is no escaping all this hype, even by bingeing out on Bing Crosby. But perhaps, this can be a reminder to us that the good news is for people in the real world; our broken, greedy, commercialized world, where the nostalgia of Christmas' past and all the razzle-dazzle of Christmas present, cannot drown out the cries of the homeless, war-torn, diseased, ravaged, impoverished, and all those suffering in countless ways.

Henry Nouwen, who taught at both Harvard and Yale and authored over forty books, spent the last seven years of his life serving in a community of people with mental disabilities. One Christmas, a member of his community arranged under the altar, three small wood-carved figures made in India: a poor woman, a poor man, and a small child between them. The carvings were simple, nearly primitive—no features, just the contours of the faces. The figures were smaller than a human hand.

But when a beam of light shone on the figures, large shadows were projected on the wall of the sanctuary. Nouwen observed how the light projected these small figures as "large, hopeful shadows against the walls of our life and world." Without the light, there was little to be seen, and one could easily pass by the figures and "continue to walk in darkness." "But," wrote Nouwen, "everything changes with the light."[1]

It is my hope that amid all the glitter, glamour, gladness, and grief of the Christmas season, you will find some shimmers of light in these spiritual reflections that will enlarge your vision of God's kingdom, expand your love for all persons, and evoke your creative participation with God's Spirit in God's project to heal and transform our world.

---

1. Nouwen, *The Genesee Diary*, 216.

1

Everyday Thankfulness

... *Shimmers of Gratitude*

At the National Prayer Breakfast in 1994 Mother Teresa said,

> One evening we went out, and we picked up four people from the street. And one of them was in a most terrible condition. I told the sisters, "You take care of the other three; I will take care of the one who looks the worst." So I did for her all that my love could do. I put her in bed, and there was such a beautiful smile on her face. She took hold of my hand as she said two words only: "Thank you." Then she died. I could not help but examine my conscience before her. And I asked, "What would I say if I were in her place? And my answer was very simple. I would have tried to draw a little attention to myself. I would have said, 'I am hungry, I am dying, I am in pain,'" ... But she gave me much more; she gave me her grateful love. And

she died with a smile on her face. Gratitude brings a smile and becomes a gift.[1]

Gratitude becomes a gift by showering its blessings on all around, but it is also engendered by a gift. *Gratitude wells up within us when we realize how precious and priceless is the gift of life.*

Unique to Luke's Gospel is a story highlighting the spiritual significance of gratitude,

> On the way to Jerusalem Jesus was going through the region between Samaria and Galilee. As he entered a village, ten lepers approached him. Keeping their distance, they called out, saying, "Jesus, Master, have mercy on us!" When he saw them, he said to them, "Go and show yourselves to the priests." And as they went, they were made clean. Then one of them, when he saw that he was healed, turned back, praising God with a loud voice. He prostrated himself at Jesus' feet and thanked him. And he was a Samaritan. Then Jesus asked, "Were not ten made clean? But the other nine, where are they? Was none of them found to return and give praise to God except this foreigner?" Then he said to him, "Get up and go on your way; your faith has made you well." Luke 17:11–19[2]

These who were healed had much for which to be thankful. Leprosy was a terrible disease. According to the Law, lepers were required to live "outside the camp" secluded

---

1. PreachingToday.com

2. Unless otherwise indicated, all Scripture quotations are from the NRSV.

and excluded from the social and religious life of the community and were required to cry, "unclean, unclean" whenever anyone approached. If a leper was fortunate enough to recover from the disease, then certification by a priest was required before he or she could reenter the community.

All the lepers healed were beneficiaries of the gift Jesus bestowed, but only one returned to express thanks to Jesus. Luke, who takes delight in favoring the marginalized, is careful to point out that the one who returned was a Samaritan. The Samaritans and the Jews were well-known for their animosity toward one another. The roots of their bitterness were deeply embedded in history; consequently, the two groups had come to believe different things and worship in different places. Also unique to Luke's Gospel is the story of the Good Samaritan. Jesus tells the story to illustrate what it means to love one's neighbor. The Samaritan stopped to help a man (presumably a Jew) who had been beaten, robbed, and left for dead, while two Jewish religious leaders passed by on the other side (Luke 10:25–37).

Luke's Gospel anticipates what is yet to come in the book of Acts, namely, a growing receptiveness to the good news among the Gentiles and a growing blindness in Israel. Israel was given a special place in God's plan for the world and yet this familiarity with the things of God did not automatically breed gratitude.

We must not, however, scapegoat the Jewish people as so many have done over the centuries. Jesus himself was a Jew, the twelve apostles were Jews, and the first church was a Jewish church. The Jesus movement began as a Jewish reform movement. Nevertheless, Luke sensed among the

Jewish people a growing rejection and blindness to the message of Christ.

But this is not merely a Jewish problem; it is a human problem. This reflects a universal condition. As Paul explains in chapter 1 of his letter to the Romans, we are all guilty of failing to acknowledge God's generous gifts (Rom 1:20–21). We all come short of honoring God fully with our lives and we all fail to express to God the gratitude God deserves.

There was once a monastery where all the brothers took a disciplined vow of total silence. They were never to speak a word; their silence was their call to listen only to God. There was, however, one exception. Once every five years, they were allowed to speak two words to the abbot who was the head of the order.

A new monk arrived at the monastery to begin his service. After five years, he went into the abbot's office to speak his two words. He said, "Food bad!" He then got up from his chair and left. Five years later, he returned to speak again. This time, his words were, "Bed hard!" And after still another five years, he returned for a third time. On his third visit he said, "Want out!" "I'm not surprised," said the abbot. "All you've done since you've been here is complain."

When we complain, when we grumble and gripe, our words feed a growing attitude of ingratitude in our hearts that is indicative of our failure to discern that God is present with us and at work among us.

Certainly there are times when it is difficult to be grateful, particularly if we are sick, dealing with some deep loss, or expending all our resources and energy just trying to survive physically, financially, or emotionally. We obviously don't feel like giving thanks in such situations and that is understandable. Yet, God has not abandoned us, even if we cannot perceive God's presence.

It is important to be sensitive to anyone who may feel disheartened and beaten down by the troubles and trials of life. I recall some years ago reading about a tornado that tore through a densely populated community. On one block, all the houses except one were completely demolished. Somehow the tornado skipped over this particular house, doing only minimal damage. When the woman of the house was interviewed, she said something to the effect, "We were so blessed." I thought then, and still think now, that her response was insensitive and arrogant.

I have no doubt that she was grateful that her house was somehow passed over, but her response lacked sensitivity and compassion for those around her. Perhaps she could have said, "We feel for and hurt with our friends and neighbors who suffered such great loss."

However, this does raise a theological question: Did God really "bless" them? Did God have anything to do with her house being spared by the tornado? I seriously doubt it. Of course, none of us are in a position to say absolutely what God may or may not do. We do not manage God. But of this I am confident: If God did have something to do with it, it was not because they had more faith or virtue than those whose houses were destroyed; it was not because of any worth, value, or merit on their part. So we need to be sensitive in the ways we express to others the gratitude we may be feeling.

But what do we do when it is our house that is decimated; when we are the ones dealing with tragedy? How do we cultivate a spirit of thanksgiving?

It is not emotionally, spiritually, or even physically healthy to deny what we actually feel. We should not pretend to feel grateful if we are not grateful. We need not be afraid to admit to God or anyone else what we honestly feel in our hearts. The Psalms are laced with a full range of intense human emotions and feelings, both negative and positive: praise, joy, and celebration, as well as bewilderment, frustration, and anger. God expects us to be honest and forthright. The Psalms show us that even when we are upset with God, racked with pain, and at the edge of despair, we can stay connected to God through our feelings of abandonment and our cries of anguish. *Our pleas for help erupting out of a deep desperation keep us in touch with God and enable us to see grace at work in the most trying of circumstances.*

Our capacity to nurture an attitude of gratitude is greatly influenced by how we "see." Luke says that the one who turned back to give Jesus thanks did so "when he saw he was healed" (17:15). The reference to "seeing" was obviously intended to imply more than physical sight. This man "saw" with a deeper wisdom; his insight sprang from a higher level of consciousness.

This is the challenge for all of us: Can we "see" beyond and through the chaotic circumstances that threaten to envelop us? Can we find some stability in God's mercy and love, even when all hell breaks loose? Can we discover the underlying thread of God's grace and presence beneath the rough, jagged texture of suffering and hardship?

I love the way Paul, in his letter to the Romans, describes God's grace that enables us to overcome the failures and hardships of life: "where sin abounds, grace does much more abound" (Rom 5:20). God's grace "out abounds" the consequences of sin—poor grammar, but excellent theology. Love will ultimately win. Redemption is God's last word. *God is large enough and great enough to absorb all the evil, tragedy, pain, and loss—reworking, reshaping, and redeeming it in due course.*

An Irish priest on a walking tour of his rural parish observed an old peasant kneeling by the side of the road, praying. Impressed, the priest said to the man, "You must be very close to God." The peasant looked up from his prayers, thought for a moment, and then smiled, "Yes, he's very fond of me." That is not arrogance; that is our birthright as human beings.

Whatever hardship or tragedy we experience, God's attitude of love toward us is constant. *To Catch an Angel*, by Robert Russell, is the autobiography of a young blind man who lived alone on an island in the middle of a river. He went rowing on the river almost everyday by means of a fairly simple system. To the end of the dock, he attached a bell with a timer set to ring every thirty seconds. In this way he was able to row up and down the river, and every thirty seconds judge his distance by the sound of the bell. When he'd had enough, he found his way home by means of the bell. In the young man's words, "The river lies before me, a constant invitation, a constant challenge, and my bell is the thread of sound along which I return to a quiet base."[3]

---

3. Referenced by Larson, *Luke*, 300.

Life is like a continually flowing river. God calls us to venture out on it where there is frequent challenge, danger, and excitement. Our security, however, rests in God's unconditional love, which enables us to find our way back home.

God's heart breaks for God's suffering children. God shares our pain. The cross of Jesus is the preeminent symbol for this in the Christian tradition. God's coming to us in Christ means that God has clothed God's self with the human condition. In the mystery of incarnation, God has taken upon God's self both the ecstasy and agony of the human plight. God knows our sufferings and feels our losses.

The Rev Henry Mitchell commented that many years ago he heard a sermon by Dr. Martin Luther King Sr. Dr. King expressed how his mother had taught him always to thank God for what is left. Everything can go wrong, but if you are left with air to breathe, be thankful. Some years later he heard Dr. King preach again, after he had lost two sons and his wife had been shot to death before his eyes at the organ in Ebenezer Church in Atlanta. Dr. King was saying the same thing, "Thank God for what is left."[4]

In spite of the darkness that had descended upon him, Dr. King was able to detect the light of God's presence and grace. *Even with all its brokenness, life is still a gift.*

This mindset was undoubtedly behind Paul's words to the church in Thessalonica, "Rejoice always, pray continually, give thanks in all circumstances; for this is God's will for you in Christ Jesus" (1 Thess 5:16–18). Paul is not instructing them to deny their pain or pretend that they do not hurt. He is not minimizing their suffering. He is ex-

---

4. PreachingToday.com.

horting them, however, to develop the discipline of "seeing" with spiritual eyes. It's possible to develop the discipline of gratitude even when we may not feel gratitude, by being aware of, attuned to, and reliant upon God's grace and abiding presence.

I love the children's story about a balloonist who was taking a trip over the Alps. His itinerary was carefully planned. But each day as he set out, something would inevitably happen to drive him off course. Instead of arriving at point A, he would find himself at point B. He always landed somewhere he hadn't planned. But each time he would say, "I didn't know this place, but this is a wonderful place. Had I known about it, I would have planned to come here."

Of course, we will not be able to say that about all the detours and setbacks that we encounter on life's journey, nor about all the tragedies and losses we experience. We cannot say that it is a wonderful place if it is not a wonderful place, but we can ask God for spiritual eyes to see God at work and to experience God's love through it all.

What would happen to us if we adopted this approach to life in the face of our disappointments and failed plans? We planned on being at one place, but we were blown off course and landed in a different place. Even though it is a hard place, a difficult place, can we discern God with us, supplying the grace we need?

If we have eyes to see, the hard place could become "a thin place," a place where the glory and goodness of God shines through. God, I think, is looking for ways to convey and communicate God's abiding presence and love. The famous Trappist monk, Thomas Merton, expressed it this way,

> Life is this simple. We are living in a world that is absolutely transparent, and God is shining through it all the time. This is not just a fable or a nice story. It is true. If we abandon ourselves to God and forget ourselves, we see it sometimes, and see it maybe frequently. God shows Himself everywhere, in everything—in people and in things and in nature and in events. It becomes very obvious that God is everywhere and in everything and we cannot be without Him. It's impossible. The only thing is that we don't see it.[5]

Perhaps it takes the wisdom, perspective, and purification of suffering to sharpen our vision and refine our spiritual senses, so that we can experience God's presence shining through the ordinary events, conversations, relationships, and experiences of our days.

Brother David Steindl–Rast tells about growing up in Nazi occupied Austria where air raids were almost a daily occurrence. On one occasion the bombs started falling just as the warning sirens began to sound, and he couldn't get to an air raid shelter. He rushed into a church a few steps away and crawled under a pew to shield himself from the falling debris and shattered glass. As the bombs exploded outside and shook the church, he felt sure the vaulted ceiling would collapse at any moment, burying him alive. When the danger passed, and surprisingly, he found himself still alive, he stepped out of the church into the midst of the smoking mounds of rubble. In the middle of all this destruction his eyes happened to fall on a few square feet of lawn that had not been touched. He said, "It was as if a friend had offered

---

5. Quoted by Borg, The *Heart of Christianity*, 155.

me an emerald in the hollow of his hand. Never before or after have I seen grass so surprisingly green."[6] His hard place became a thin place.

Jesus' final words to the restored leper are significant, "Get up and go on your way; your faith has made you well" (Luke 17:19). Obviously this means more than, "Your faith has healed you." The word translated "made you well" can also be translated "saved you" or "made you whole." This is something "more" than physical healing; it is a deeper, spiritual wholeness that can only be experienced through gratitude. How could it be possible to be spiritually mature without a spirit of gratitude in our lives?

We can find reasons for being either grateful or bitter. We have to determine the attitude that will permeate our minds and hearts. Henry Nouwen, who eventually gave up a distinguished teaching position at Yale University to work with developmentally disabled adults, has commented how he saw these decisions at work in his community every day. Men and women with mental and physical disabilities have every reason to be bitter. They experience loneliness, rejection from family members and friends, the unfulfilled desire to have a partner in life, and the constant frustration of continually needing assistance. And yet, said Nouwen, most do not choose to be bitter, but "grateful for the many small gifts of their lives—for an invitation to dinner, for a few days of retreat or a birthday celebration, and most of all, for their daily community with people who offer friendship and support."[7] For many of their assistants who worked with them daily, they became a source of hope and

6. Steindl-Rast, *Gratefulness, the Heart of Prayer*, 10.
7. Quoted by Thomas, *The Glorious Pursuit*, 145.

inspiration. Nouwen observed that gratitude had a way of begetting more gratitude and love begetting more love. *The more we decide to be grateful, the easier it becomes to live a grateful life.*

Even when our problems seem unsolvable and our mountains unclimbable, God is with us. As we cultivate an attitude of gratitude for God's sustaining and supporting grace amid all the tensions and pressures of life's trials, and as we learn to live through our disappointments and let go of our frustrations, then we will become more aware and alive, more whole and complete— more fully human. Our hard places may become thin places where we can catch a glimpse of God's glory and grace.

2

Advent's Invitation

... Shimmers of Hope

MANY OF us get caught up in a flurry of activities this time of year, so what should be a time of renewal becomes a season of burgeoning stress. The "holiday season" can send some of us on a roller coaster ride of emotions. One minute we are eager and excited about getting together with our family and friends; the next moment we feel lonely, sad, and angry.

Even those of us who truly love Christmas often miss the point. Too many Christians are content with candles and carols and the security of familiar family traditions and gatherings. These are all good things, but even good things can become a distraction, keeping us from experiencing the best thing.

"Advent" is derived from a Latin word meaning "arrival" or "coming." Advent marks something momentous: Christ's coming into our midst. We generally think of Advent as a celebration of a past event, the Christ-Event, as expressed by the litany in First Timothy 3:16,

> Beyond all question, the mystery of godliness is great: He appeared in a body, was vindicated by the Spirit, was seen by angels, was preached among the nations, was believed on in the world, was taken up in glory. (NIV)

Many Christians also think of Advent as a future event, a coming anticipated, a second advent. I would like to suggest that we may also think of Advent as a present and ongoing experience. The "mystery of godliness," the mystery of advent, of incarnation, is something that is continually unfolding, pressing upon us, encouraging and uplifting us in our disappointments and trials, but also confronting and challenging us in our false securities and allegiances.

I love the story about the little girl who came running out of her room after a particularly loud crack of thunder and bright flash of lightning. She jumped in bed with her parents and exclaimed, "Mommy, I'm scared." Her mother reassured her that everything would be all right, offering words of comfort, "Remember honey, God is with you." She replied, "I know, but I really want someone with skin on his face."

Advent invites us to stand in awe before the God who became incarnate in human flesh; a God with "skin on his face." "The mystery of godliness," says the sacred text, "was vindicated by the Spirit." The mention of vindication is undoubtedly a reference to Christ's resurrection. His resurrection served as God's vindication of his life and death. God, in raising Jesus from the dead, validated Jesus' message of God's new world (the kingdom of God on earth) and affirmed his compassionate self-giving for the good of others, even unto death.

God's Spirit is still vindicating and validating "the mystery of godliness" as the Spirit bears witness to our spirit, as deep calls to deep. Paul wrote to the Galatian churches,

> But when the set time had fully come, God sent his Son, born of a woman, born under the law, to redeem those under the law, that we might receive adoption to sonship. Because you are his sons, God sent the Spirit of his Son into our hearts, the Spirit who calls out, *Abba*, Father." (Gal 4:4–6)

The Spirit illumines, reveals, and mediates the living presence of Christ, affirming and validating our identity as children of God.

In Luke's Gospel the angel says to Mary, "The Holy Spirit will come upon you and the power of the Most High will overshadow you. So the holy one to be born will be called the Son of God" (Luke 1:35). Mary responds, "I am the Lord's servant . . . May it be to me according to your word" (Luke 1:38). In her submission, relinquishment, and obedience to God's purpose, Christ was conceived.

And so it is for all of us. In our surrender, relinquishment, and obedience to God's will, we experience the living Christ as the Son of God. To know Jesus as "Son of God" is to experience Christ as Savior (Liberator and Deliverer). In Luke's Gospel, the angel announced to the shepherds, "Do not be afraid; for see—I am bringing you good news of great joy for all the people; to you is born this day in the city of David a Savior, who is the Messiah, the Lord" (Luke 2:10–11). In Israel's tradition, the designation "Son of God" was used to refer to angels, kings, prophets, as well as the just and wise. These were all persons (or angels) anointed and set apart to mediate God's presence and accomplish God's will in some special way. We experience Christ as "Son of God" through his revelation of God and mediation of salvation.

Personal salvation is never fully attained by anyone in this life. It is a process of conversion that, like the energizer bunny, goes on and on. As we open our lives to the truth and light of Christ, the dark parts of our personality and ego are exposed. Christ, then, is able to begin the process of rescuing us from the deception and tyranny of our false selves, helping us to break free from our personal addictions and group idolatries. As Christ works redemptively in us, we discover some measure of freedom from the pride, arrogance, greed, anger, bitterness, ignorance, and narrowness that threatens our relationships, as well as the health and well–being of our very lives.

Time and again the living Christ reveals himself in redeeming grace. One of the ways his transforming presence reaches us is through the Spirit at work in the church, his body. We encounter Christ in community in ways that are not available to us in isolation.

A young woman started participating in a small, country Presbyterian church and presented her child for baptism, a child conceived outside of marriage. The day of the baptism the woman stood alone before the congregation, holding her child in her arms. The pastor hadn't recognized the awkwardness of the situation. He came to that part of the baptismal service when the questions are asked, "Who stands with this child to assure the commitments and promises herewith made will be carried out? Who will be there for this child in times of need and assure that this child is brought up in the nurture and admonition of the Lord?" It was then that he realized there was no godmother or godfather on hand to answer the question. But without hesitation, as though on cue, the entire congregation stood and with one voice said, "We will!"[1] This is Christ present and visible in his body; the mystery of godliness at work in and through the people of God.

We also encounter Christ in the everydayness of life. Some of these experiences are quite extraordinary; others are rather routine and mundane, yet they glisten with the radiance of God's Spirit. I have had experiences where I became keenly aware of and passionately moved by God in the most common of circumstances and ordinary of places. Many of these encounters have come at times when I least expected them: in a casual conversation with a friend, while wading in a local creek fishing for smallmouth bass, on a brisk Saturday morning walk with my wife, in the emergency room waiting on news about a parishioner. *God is present in all of our experiences, especially in times of great suffering.*

Clarence Jordan, the founder of Koinonia Farm in Americus, Georgia, makes the point in one of his sermons that God raised Jesus from the dead, not as an invitation for us to come to heaven when we die, but as a declaration that God has established permanent residence on earth. The resurrection, argues Jordan, was not primarily God's way of showing us that there is life after death; rather, it places Jesus on this side of the grave, here and now, in the midst of life. "He is not standing on the shore of eternity beckoning

1. Campolo, *Let Me Tell You a Story*, 164.

us to join him there. He is standing beside us, strengthening us in this life."[2]

The Spirit at work in the church and in the "everydayness" of life offers us glimpses into the kind of world Jesus proclaimed when he announced that the kingdom of God was at hand, the kind of world that the Spirit is presently creating.

A minister was preparing his sermon in his study at home. His little daughter stormed in and said, "Daddy, can we play?" He responded, "I'm sorry, sweetheart, I'm in the middle of getting my sermon ready for Sunday. We'll play later this afternoon." She sighed, "Okay" and then declared, "When you're finished, I'm going to give you a big hug." She turned to leave, but when she got to the door, she spun around, raced back to her father, reached up and gave him a bone-breaking embrace. He said, "Honey, I thought you were going to give me the hug later when I finished." She said, "I am. I just wanted you to know what you have to look forward to."

In our present day experiences of Advent, where we see the face of God in a little child, or when we witness God's love expressed in a daring act of forgiveness, or when we embrace an enemy who becomes a friend, we are endowed with *a preview of God's new world*, a glimpse of the coming kingdom.

Tony Campolo tells about being in front of a television in a hotel in Zurich, Switzerland. He was between flights on his way home from Africa. As he watched, some pictures flashed on the screen of the closing celebration of the Olympic Games. At first, the teams, wearing their official

2. Jordan, *The Substance of Faith*, 26.

uniforms and carrying their national flags, marched around the stadium in a structured parade that looked like soldiers on review. But then suddenly the Olympians broke ranks. They ran and danced with one another in a spontaneous outpouring of enthusiasm. The neat columns that defined people groups disappeared. Nationalistic identities no longer mattered. No longer were there winners and losers, rich and poor, one nationality and another—just human beings dancing, hugging, laughing, and celebrating life together. In that moment, all divisions between the races and people groups were eradicated as they danced together in joyful celebration.[3]

In these experiences of grace, where the inclusive love of God pierces through all the darkness of human exclusion and division, we get a taste of the future banquet where all are guests of honor.

Jesus' life in this world began in a small, one-room peasant house that would have been divided into living quarters and space for the animals. Jesus was placed as a baby in a feeding trough. It was most likely cold, damp, and dirty, not the kind of warm, cozy place often pictured in our contemporary manger scenes. His life ended on a cross between two criminals. Jesus was born in humility and died in humiliation. Brennan Manning writes, "God entered into our world not with the crushing impact of unbearable glory, but in the way of weakness, vulnerability, and need. On a wintry night in an obscure cave, the infant Jesus was a humble, naked, helpless God who allowed us to get close to him."[4] Yet, this

3. Campolo, *The Kingdom of God Is a Party*, 44.
4. Manning, "Shipwrecked at the Stable," 187.

same Jesus boldly confronted the abuse and injustice wielded by the powers that be without fear or trepidation.

This is not all that marketable: a weak, vulnerable God who comes to us as a teacher of wisdom, a sage, a healer and prophet, who challenges the status quo, turning conventional wisdom on its head and the kingdoms of the world upside down. How many versions of American Christianity muzzle Jesus' roar, leaving us with "a tame lion"?[5] Some of these approaches trim off Jesus' rough edges so he can be neatly packaged for a culture obsessed with comfort and security. Whether it's health and wealth in this life or the afterlife, some folks want a Jesus who can solve all their problems, answer all their questions, and be an endless source of comfort and happiness. Jesus, however, ends up on a cross and he bids his disciples to follow the same path.

In his book, *Letters to My Children*, Daniel Taylor tells about an experience he had in the sixth grade. Periodically the students were taught to dance, and in those days the teacher would line up the boys at the door of the classroom to choose their partners. Thankfully, this sort of thing is not done anymore. Imagine being one of the girls waiting to be chosen, and being passed by.

One girl named Mary was always chosen last. A childhood illness left her disabled. She was neither pretty nor smart. The assistant teacher happened to attend Taylor's church and she pulled him aside one day and said, "Dan, next time we have dancing, I want you to choose Mary; it's what Jesus would do." He couldn't believe she asked him to do this. The next time they had dancing, he struggled with

---

5. The phrase, "no tame lion" is a phrase used by C. S. Lewis in the Chronicles of Narnia to describe Aslan, the Christ figure.

what to do. He hoped he would be last in line so he would have to choose Mary, but instead it turned out that he was the first in line.

As he looked at the faces of the girls before him, the pretty ones smiling, fully expecting to be chosen first, he noticed that Mary was the only one half-turned away. She had experienced rejection so many times that she knew she would not be picked. So what would he do? He says, "I remember feeling very far away. I heard my voice say, 'I choose Mary.'" Taylor writes, "Never has reluctant virtue been so rewarded . . . Today I can still see her beaming face, fixated with surprise and pleasure and delight at being chosen . . . I had to look away because I knew I didn't deserve it."[6]

We meet Christ among "the least." Of course, "the least" are only "the least" from the point of view of a world gone awry, a world that elevates wealth and status over humility and compassion, a world that rewards the winners and the successful. Jesus turns this sort of world upside down. Jesus says, "Blessed are you who are poor, for yours is the kingdom of God. Blessed are you who are hungry now, for you will be filled. Blessed are you who weep now, for you will laugh. Blessed are you when people hate you, and when they exclude you, revile you, and defame you on account of the Son of Man" (Luke 6:20–22). This is a whole different perspective, isn't it?

In Mary's Song of Praise (Magnificat) the proud are scattered and the powerful deposed, while the humble are lifted up and the weak strengthened. The rich are stripped of their wealth and the hungry are filled with good things

6. Referenced by Yaconelli, *Messy Spirituality*, 84–85.

(Luke 1:51–53). A change of fortunes is anticipated in the Messianic age.

God's choice of a humble peasant girl to give birth to the Messiah signals that the great eschatological reversal has already commenced. God's values and the world's values clash in a collision of opposites. To partner with Christ in the work of the kingdom is to side with the powerless and the oppressed, for to them belongs God's new world.

God's favor rests upon the poor, weak, powerless, and humble. Unless we find ourselves among them, we will not likely encounter Christ's presence and experience his salvation.

This "mystery of godliness" is not only difficult to market, it is difficult to comprehend. Just as a humble attitude is necessary in matters of the heart, so it is equally true in matters of the mind. Author Madeleine L'Engle exclaims, "Don't try to explain the Incarnation to me! It is further from being explainable than the furthest star in the furthest galaxy. It is love, God's limitless love enfleshing that love into the form of a human being, Jesus, the Christ, fully human and fully divine."[7]

Any rendering of Christianity that reduces "the mystery of godliness" to a propositional statement, a creed, or doctrinal formula diminishes its truth. Any attempt to explain it will inevitably miss the mark and stifle spiritual understanding. One needs a healthy and lively imagination to approach the mystery of the incarnation.

The coming of God in Christ invites us to bow in wonder and entertain the mystery in a spirit of humility and awe. Clarence Jordan has pointed out that in our deifica-

7. L'Engle, "A Sky Full of Children," 80.

tion of Jesus we have effectively made him irrelevant. When God becomes like us, we are not sure what to do with him. As long as God stays God, then we can keep our distance. We can sing songs of praise to God and build our cathedrals to honor him. Jordan tells of a church in Georgia that spent thousands of dollars building a granite fountain on the church lawn that circulated water to the tune of one thousand gallons a second. Jordan remarks, "Now that ought to be enough to satisfy any Baptist. But what on earth is a church doing taking God Almighty's money in a time of great need like this and setting up a little old fountain on its lawn to bubble water around? I was thirsty . . . and ye built me a fountain. We can handle God as long as he stays God. We can build him a fountain. But when he becomes a man we have to give him a cup of water. So the virgin birth is simply the great transcendent truth that God Almighty has come into the affairs of man and dwells among us."[8]

When Jesus set forth his agenda in terms of Isaiah 61:1–2 in the synagogue in Nazareth, with all eyes fastened on him, he announced, "Today this scripture has been fulfilled in your hearing" (Luke 4:21). Jesus inaugurated the Messianic age and his Spirit is presently with us, among us, and in us, pointing us to the kingdom of God and drawing us into this God Movement of love, justice, and peace in the world.

Author and former pastor, Bruce Larson tells about living on a little island in Florida that had a well-known restaurant called, "Scotty's Pub." Outside the pub was a sign promising "free beer tomorrow." Larson says he lived there for six years and in all that time not a drop of free

8. Jordan, *Substance of Faith*, 15.

beer was dispensed. If the promise is always for free beer tomorrow, then there is no free beer today. Some expressions of Christianity leave the impression that all we have to offer is pie-in-the-sky, bye-and-bye—which Jesus said practically nothing about. When Jesus taught the disciples to pray he said nothing about going to heaven, but instructed them to pray that God's kingdom, God's new world, would come to earth.

Advent is more than a memory of what took place in the past or an expectation of what is to occur in the future. Certainly Advent's invitation includes both remembrance and anticipation, but the light that was and will be *is now*, shimmering against the backdrop of our existence. The *presence* of Christ is for the *present*.

The invitation of Advent is the invitation—right now, this very moment—to open our ordinary lives, common experiences, and everyday relationships, as well as our deepest selves, to the Spirit of the living Christ. Today is the day of salvation. Today is the day the Lord has made, let us be glad and give ourselves to it, to live in it as one fully alive, with eyes wide open. Advent is now!

3

Awakenings

. . . Shimmers of Renewal

CHRISTMAS IS a season glimmering with dazzling displays and decorations. I am particularly drawn to trees glistening with tinsel, ribbon, and sparkling ornaments. Another feature I especially like are the many colorful and varied light arrangements adorning yards, trees, houses, city streets and parks. Many churches have a "Hanging of the Green" service to kick off Advent when the church is decorated with evergreens, chrismons, unique advent banners, manger scenes, candles of all sizes and shapes, and of course, the central piece of the advent liturgy, the advent wreath. There is much to see.

A foundational characteristic of a healthy, transformational spiritual life is our capacity to see. When I make this point with church groups I like to illustrate with two stories. I begin by saying, "Perhaps a story will illustrate. There was a farmer who had a barn and it burned down. So he built another barn, and a storm blew it down. So he decided to build a better barn, one built entirely out of brick—brick floor, brick walls, brick roof, thousands and thousands of bricks. When he finished he had one brick left over. He stood there contemplating that one brick. What do you think he did with that one brick? He threw the brick over his shoulder and walked away." At this point I pause and smile, waiting for a response. Then I repeat with emphasis, "He threw the brick over his shoulder and walked away!" Again, I pause, waiting for a response. Then I say, "You don't get it do you? Melissa (my wife) told me not to tell that story. She said it's a silly story and no one would get the point. As much as I hate to make this admission, she was right; I should have listened to her."

Next I say, "Let me try again. There was a woman riding a train, and she had a dog she liked very much; so much that she purchased a seat right beside her for her dog to ride in. The man in front of her was smoking a foul–smelling cigar, and the smoke was drifting back into the face of the dog. The little dog was having a hard time with this. The woman tapped the man on the shoulder and asked, 'Would you mind extinguishing your cigar? It's bothering my dog.'

The man said, 'Madame, there are non-smoking cars on this train and there are smoking cars. This is a smoking car. I will continue to enjoy my cigar.' Well, by this time the little dog was coughing and panting, so she tapped him on the shoulder again and asked him once more to please put out his cigar. Again, he refused. Now the little dog started turning blue. In desperation, the woman reached over, opened the window, then whipped around and yanked the cigar out of the man's mouth and tossed it out. The man, in response, very calmly but quickly, before the woman could react, picked up her dog and threw the dog out the window.

Awakenings 27

The woman went into hysterics and started pounding her fists on the man's back.

Just then the train slowed down and came to a stop at the station. The woman hurried down the platform and just as she reached the bottom step, her little dog came running up to her. And guess what the dog had in his mouth?" After a long pause I say, "He had the brick the farmer threw over his shoulder." I conclude, "Now the first story makes sense doesn't it? Well, sort of anyway. You see the big picture. The first story now makes sense in light of the second story. As Christians we make sense out of life, we see the big picture, in light of the story of Jesus."

In John chapter 3, Jesus tells the Pharisee Nicodemus, who came to him by night, "Very truly, I tell you, no one can see the kingdom of God without being born from above" (John 3:3). The Greek word translated "born from above" has a double meaning; it can also be translated "born anew" (or "again"). Jesus is in effect saying, "Unless you come to see with new eyes, you will not be able to 'see'—to grasp, to understand, to experience, to know—the kingdom of God." *Life in the kingdom of God depends on our capacity to see.*

What does Jesus/John mean by the kingdom of God? The phrase carries a lot of baggage and rather than attempt to unpack it all, here is one description: The kingdom of God is present wherever God is in charge; where God is at work healing what is sick and broken, making right what has gone awry, and reconciling all things to God's self and to one another. In the Gospels, it is a rather dynamic and fluid symbol that has earthly, social, relational, spiritual, and political implications. It's about forgiveness, reconciliation, peace, healing, and justice in our personal lives, relationships, communities, society, and the world.

Imagine what the world would look like if God were in charge. Most of us who are followers of Christ anticipate a day when God's peace and righteousness, God's good intent for the planet and for humankind will prevail—when the oppressed will be liberated, poverty abolished, evil redeemed, and all creation made right and whole. It's almost too good to hope for isn't it? We may hold to different versions on how this will come to pass, but unlike the characters in a Woody Allen film, we do not feel that life is meaningless or that death is all there is. We trust that life is going somewhere. As disciples of Jesus we believe that Jesus proclaimed and embodied the redeeming reality of the kingdom through his words, deeds, death, and resurrection, and that the Spirit of the living Christ is present with us, among us, and in us, interacting with our world in transformative love and grace. *As Christians we experience this dynamic, renewing and life-enhancing reality of the kingdom through our friendship and partnership with the living Christ.*

God is at work in our world, even though God's work is often hidden like yeast in bread dough. The presence of the Spirit of the living Christ can take many different forms, shapes, and expressions. Sometimes (perhaps many times) those of us who should see, even those of us who are steeped in religious traditions, do not see and we need the fresh wind of the Spirit to blow away the scales that cover our eyes so that we can see anew.

Nicodemus was a leader in Judaism, heir to a rich tradition of spiritual wisdom, and Jesus expected him to be able to grasp what he was saying. When Nicodemus expressed his lack of understanding, Jesus said, "Are you a teacher of Israel and yet you do not understand these things?" (John 3:10)

In his conversation with Nicodemus, Jesus used the imagery of birth to talk about the necessity of spiritual insight, understanding, and change. Christ's message can be paraphrased as follows: Unless we have a new birth, a birth from above—an awakening, a new vision, a new way of assessing, understanding, and knowing reality—then we will not "see" or "enter" God's kingdom. We will not understand, experience, or be free to participate in God's new world. It's not that God will intentionally exclude us from participating; rather, it is simply that we will not have the aptitude and capacity for experiencing it.

Franciscan priest and author, Richard Rohr employs a wonderful image that helps us "see" the big picture; he calls this "the cosmic egg of meaning."[1] He describes three expanding domes or levels of meaning. The first dome he names "My story." This is the story of our personal, private lives. No other people in the history of civilization have been able to live so fully at this level of meaning as we have in the western world over the last century. This is the language of "talk shows" where personal interests, tastes, desires, and aspirations dominate.

We all have a personal story, and most of us are grateful that we have so much freedom to choose the direction and course of our personal stories. But we can easily get trapped at this level of meaning, and we all do to one de-

---

1. I am especially indebted to Rohr here. See his image and explanation in *Hope Against Darkness*, 83–96.

gree or another. Our lives can become consumed by ego needs and desires, and with the pursuit of position, power, prestige, or possessions. When we become enslaved to our selfish agenda life becomes "all about me"—people become objects we use for our own benefit. We become absorbed in the endless game of comparison and competition that operates at every level of society. Driven by our ego needs, we feel that we have to win, that we have to climb the ladder of success, that we have to be seen or recognized for our achievements. There are a lot of pitfalls here and Jesus certainly had these things in mind when he said, "One must lose his or her life in order to find life."

The second dome of meaning (which encompasses the first) is what Rohr labels "Our story." This is the sphere of group identity and loyalty, which encompasses our family, tribe, people, religion, group, and nation. Here too, we can easily become entangled in the web of group identities and loyalties in ways that are harmful and destructive to ourselves and others. Our commitment can devolve blindly into, "my country, my religion, my family, my political party, my team, my group whether right or wrong, good or bad." Our sense of identity can be so tied and bound to a group that we become incapable of exercising critical discernment and simply fall in line like robots.

This happens quite frequently. There are Republicans and Democrats who have lost all ability and freedom to criticize their own party because their identity and security are so yoked to the group. There are Christian leaders, pastors, and church members who have lost all freedom and capacity to constructively criticize their denomination, church, or doctrine because of their unhealthy attachment to the group. We can become so dependent upon the group for our sense of who we are, for our self-worth, that we lose the capacity to discern and question what is good or evil, what is healthy or unhealthy, what is helpful or harmful.

Even our personal identities can become so absorbed in our group identities that we lose the capacity to self-criticize, to admit when we are wrong, to confess our failures, and to make course corrections. Any of us, at any time, can become entrapped at either of these two levels of meaning.

Rohr calls the third dome of meaning (which encompasses the previous two), "The story." At this level we encounter the great universal patterns and truths that lead to real transformation. These relational and lifestyle patterns nurture the great virtues like faith, humility, unconditional love, compassion, courage, and hope, leading to personal and communal healing, forgiveness, peace, reconciliation, solidarity with the suffering and oppressed, and an inclusive vision that embraces all people as children of God. These great universal patterns empower people to make redemptive choices, to be good stewards of the creation, and to live as agents of transformation.

This is what Jesus called the kingdom of God. As we live in this dome of reality we experience real freedom and soul growth. The more we embrace these universal redemptive patterns the more freedom we have to recognize, name, and let go of our personal addictions and group idolatries. *Living in the kingdom of God frees us from the selfish ambitions and ego desires of our personal stories, as well as the destructive biases, prejudices, and injustices of our group identities.*

The biblical tradition recognizes the importance of all three domes of reality, but our participation in the larger dome, the kingdom of God, is necessary to bring balance and wholeness to our personal and group stories. As we adopt and appropriate these transformative patterns of unconditional love, justice, forgiveness, service, humility, and compassion, we experience psychic and emotional (sometimes physical) healing, spiritual and relational growth, and habitual change in various aspects of our lives.

When we live in this third dome of reality, we are living in the Spirit. The Spirit opens our eyes so that we can see. *The Spirit is the redemptive power of the kingdom of God,* actively inspiring and leading us into these universal transformative patterns.

Religion itself is not the answer. Nicodemus was a religious professional, but he was spiritually blind. Jesus said to him, "If I have told you about earthly things and you do not believe, how can you believe if I tell you about heavenly things?" (John 3:12) "Earthly" and "heavenly," in the above context, do not refer to separate spheres of reality, but to degrees of reality. Jesus is asking, "If you do not understand the basics of life in God's kingdom, how will you grasp true spiritual reality?" He needed the equivalent of a new birth, a birth from above, an immersion in the Spirit of God, an awakening. He needed new eyes. We all do, so that we can experience this third dome of reality—the universal patterns that heal and transform life.

Life in the kingdom of God brings harmony and balance to everything else. Jesus told his disciples to seek first the kingdom of God and God's righteousness/justice (the great universal patterns for a flourishing life, community, and world), and everything else would fall into place (Matt 6:33).

This is what healthy Christianity (or healthy religion, for that matter) does for us. It enables us to experience life in God's kingdom. It opens our lives to the Divine Spirit, allowing the Spirit access to our deepest self. As Jesus points out in his conversation with Nicodemus, we cannot manipulate or manage the Spirit. The Spirit is as free as the wind; the Spirit blows where it will. We cannot coerce or force the Spirit's action, but we can invite and welcome the Spirit into our hearts, our relationships, and into the nitty-gritty of our common and uncommon lives.

One of the ways we open our lives to the Spirit and prepare for the Spirit's movement is through what the biblical tradition calls repentance. *Repentance is the pathway into these universal patterns of the kingdom of God.*

The Synoptic Gospels all declare that John the Baptist, the forerunner of the Messiah, proclaimed a baptism of repentance in the desert of Judea. He called the exiled people of God to renewal in preparation for the realization of the kingdom of God. John proclaimed his message with a sense of urgency and immediacy. Evidently he saw himself living on the edge of the fullness of time, the edge of fulfillment. Undoubtedly influenced by apocalyptic thought, John announced that the judgment preceding the time of fulfillment was upon them. John said to the crowds that came out to be baptized by him,

> "You brood of vipers! Who warned you to flee from the wrath to come? Bear fruits worthy of repentance. Do not begin to say to yourselves, 'We have Abraham as our ancestor'; for I tell

you, God is able from these stones to raise up children to Abraham. Even now the ax is lying at the root of the trees; every tree therefore that does not bear good fruit is cut down and thrown into the fire." . . . As the people were filled with expectation, and all were questioning in their hearts concerning John, whether he might be the Messiah, John answered all of them by saying, "I baptize you with water; but one who is more powerful than I is coming; I am not worthy to untie the thong of his sandals. He will baptize you with the Holy Spirit and fire. His winnowing fork is in his hand, to clear his threshing floor and to gather the wheat into his granary; but the chaff he will burn with unquenchable fire." Luke 3:7–9, 15–17

While we may not share John's sense of temporal urgency, we can share his sense of immediacy. The kingdom of God is here, among us and within us. The transformative, redemptive love of the Spirit is blowing at will, wooing us, convicting us, inviting us, and drawing us toward God's self, calling us to participate in these universal patterns of forgiveness, peace, justice, and grace.

If we look at the above text through a dualistic lens, our interpretations can easily become just another way for us to circle our wagons in defense of our personal stories and group identities, and to feel complacent in our certitudes by dividing humanity into "us" and "them," "saved" and "unsaved," "good" and "evil," "wheat" and "chaff." Have you ever noticed that whenever we engage in this sort of dualistic exegesis that we are always the ones on the inside? Dualistic interpreters inevitably see themselves as the insiders, the saved, the righteous, or the ones who have the truth. And if the "chaff" on the outside will just join our group, adopt our beliefs, and conform to our version of the truth, then they too can be "saved" and "blessed."

If, however, we read this Scripture on a different level, through an inclusivistic lens, through our common humanity and common identity as the children of God (I'll say more about this in the next chapter), then this text provides some wonderfully rich soil in which to grow our souls. We are all a mixed bag of wheat and chaff. No one is all "wheat" or all "chaff."

The fire, of course, is a symbol of the Spirit and while we do not take it literally, we should take it seriously. The text reminds us that we must all undergo a baptism of fire—the refining work of the Spirit—and "repentance" is part of the process. The Spirit as fire burns away the chaff in our lives and baptizes us into these great patterns of love and justice. This baptism (immersion, saturation) in the Spirit consumes the prejudice, greed, and evil in us, empowering us to walk in the way of humility, love, truth, and peace.

The Spirit exposes the "chaff" while providing the courage to face it, rather than deny, ignore, or repress it. The Spirit enables us to hold the tension, to bear this collision of opposites, without yielding to either of two temptations—self-negation (self-contempt) or self-deception (illusion). The Spirit enables us to be painfully honest as we admit our failures, flaws, sins, and illusions, while assuring us that we are God's precious and beloved children.

Author Sue Monk Kid tells about finding an old bundle of Christmas cards while poking around in the attic looking for a picture frame. She sat down under the exposed light bulb dangling from the rafter and sifted through them. Halfway through the stack she found a card that had meant a great deal to her one year. She was seven months pregnant, terribly tired of waiting, and yearning to hold her baby in her arms. The days seemed to drag by. Then the card came. On the front was Mary, great with child, and inside were the words, "Let it be."

The words come from Luke 1:38, which is Mary's response to the angel who told her that she would give birth to God's Son, "Here I am, the servant of the Lord; let it be with me according to your word." With these words, says Kidd, "she (Mary) let go of her own will and the security of her old way of life and yielded to the purposes of God."[2] Kidd felt a kinship with Mary; she felt as if Mary had come to show her how to wait through her pregnancy. Kidd writes, "Don't fret so, the card seemed to say. You can't control the life in you. It grows and emerges in its own time. Be patient and nurture it with all your love and attentiveness. Be still and cooperate with the mystery God is unfolding in you. *Let it be*."[3]

True repentance involves a letting go of our old identities, securities, and fears, and a surrendering to the Spirit who is at work forming Christ in us. We cannot control the growth of the Christ-life within us, but we can patiently nurture it and seek to cooperate with God's Spirit who is shaping us into Christ's image. Paul said to the Galatians, "I have been crucified with Christ; and it is no longer I [the ego/false self, the little self with its false attachments and group biases] who live, but it is Christ who lives in me" (Gal

2. Kidd, *When the Heart Waits*, 111
3. Ibid., 110–11.

2:19b–20). To live in Christ and to have Christ live in us is to live in the mystery, beauty, and largeness of "The Story." Repentance is a process. We are prone to fall back into old patterns of ego desire, personal addictions, and group idolatries, and so *we must be born again and again and again.* The Spirit, who leads us in this pilgrimage, frees us to move forward, changing us "from one degree of glory to another" (2 Cor 3:17–18).

Unique to Luke's Gospel is John's counsel to the people who came to be baptized,

> And the crowds asked him, "What then should we do?" In reply he said to them, "Whoever has two coats must share with anyone who has none; and whoever has food must do likewise." Even tax collectors came to be baptized, and they asked him, "Teacher, what should we do?" He said to them, "Collect no more than the amount prescribed for you." Soldiers also asked him, "And we, what should we do?" He said to them, "Do not extort money from anyone by threats or false accusations, and be satisfied with your wages." Luke 3:10–14

No one is beyond the rim. The wideness of God's mercy embraces all. No one is excluded. Not the despised tax collectors, who were traitors and conspirators with Rome in their oppressive tax system, nor even the greedy, violent Roman soldiers.

The "fruits of repentance" specifically mentioned above were those of particular significance to the people addressed. The common people who were oppressed beneath the heavy tax burden of Rome and reduced to poverty were told to share with one another out of their resources. The tax collectors were instructed to be honest and forthright, while the soldiers were told to be content with their wages and treat others fairly.

Authentic repentance is always expressed in concrete, tangible ways. Author Brennan Manning shares how the late Rich Mullins taught him an invaluable lesson about the meaning of true repentance. "One rainy day," says Manning, "he [Rich] got into a blistering argument with his road manager, Gay Quisenberry. Angry words were hurled back and forth, and Rich stormed out the door, uncontrite. Early the following morning, Gay was awakened from a sound sleep by the loud buzz of a motor outside her house. Groggily, she looked out the window and saw Rich mowing her lawn!"[4]

As we "bear fruits worthy of repentance," as we share with those in need, live humbly and practice honesty, as we forgive one another and sow seeds of kindness and mercy, we are opening our lives to the transforming power of the Spirit and participating in God's new world. The more we manifest the fruits of repentance, the more open and attentive we become to the movement and redemptive love of the Spirit.

This is our part. *To be open, ready, and receptive to the wind and fire of the Spirit*, to engage in these universal attitudinal, relational, and lifestyle patterns that make for a rich, flourishing personal and communal life. The Spirit is blowing at will. We cannot control it, but we can hoist the sails and catch the wind. As we learn to live in the dynamic love of God's kingdom, all the other components that constitute the stuff of our lives will fall into place.

4. Smith, *Rich Mullins*, xiii.

4

The Way of Peace

... Shimmers of a World Made Whole

By the tender mercy of our God, the dawn from on high will break upon us, to give light to those who sit in darkness and in the shadow of death, to guide our feet into the way of peace.

—Luke 1:78–79[1]

WHAT ARE your first thoughts when asked to reflect on the word "peace"? You might think of a feeling of ease or comfort. The popular country rock group, the Eagles, had a hit song that echoed the heart's longing for a "peaceful, easy feeling." As you anticipate family gatherings this season one of your Christmas wishes may be: "I hope we have a peaceful time with family this year." Invariably, there is always someone in the family who knows what hot buttons to push to get uncle or aunt so-and-so on his or her soapbox. Or you might think of a pastoral scene, like the one reflected in Psalm 23, "He makes me lie down in green pastures; he leads

---

1. While the previous lines of Zechariah's prophecy refer to his son, John, these concluding lines speak of the Messiah.

me beside the still waters." Sometimes peace is depicted in negative terms, such as the absence of strife or conflict. The biblical meaning is much broader and deeper.

In the Greek world, "peace" was often employed to describe an inner state of well-being, whereas in the Hebrew tradition, the word was used primarily "for interpersonal or social relations where it comes very close to meaning 'justice.'"[2] Both of these perspectives are found in the New Testament, and though a particular context may emphasize one or the other meaning, neither meaning should exclude the other.

In a Peanuts cartoon Lucy says to Charlie Brown, "I hate everything. I hate everybody. I hate the whole wide world." Charlie Brown responds, "But I thought you had inner peace." Lucy replies, "I do have peace. But I still have outer obnoxiousness." Whatever Lucy may have, it is not spiritual peace. In the biblical tradition, inner peace goes hand-in-hand with relational and communal wholeness.

In the birth narrative of Luke's Gospel we read,

> In that region there were shepherds living in the fields, keeping watch over their flock by night. Then an angel of the Lord stood before them, and the glory of the Lord shone around them, and they were terrified. But the angel said to them, "Do not be afraid; for see—I am bringing you good news of great joy for all the people: to you is born this day in the city of David a Savior, who is the Messiah, the Lord. This will be a sign for you: you will find a child wrapped in bands of cloth and lying in a manger." And suddenly there

2. Larsen, "Peace," 213.

> was with the angel a multitude of the heavenly host, praising God and saying, "Glory to God in the highest heaven, and on earth peace among those whom he favors!" (Luke 2:10–14)

In the Roman Empire, it was customary for poets and orators to proclaim peace and prosperity at the birth of one who was destined to become emperor. Following that familiar pattern, the angelic messenger announces the birth of Christ, the Lord, who is destined to be the Savior of Israel and the world. The irony is that Israel's Messiah and Deliverer is Rome's Savior as well.

Luke begins the actual birth story by setting it in the historical context of Emperor Augustus. Caesar Augustus was heralded as the greatest of the emperors. He was born Octavian and was the adopted son of Julius Caesar. Following his father's assassination a great civil war tore Rome asunder, wrecking havoc on the empire until Octavian defeated Mark Antony and Cleopatra in 31 BCE at the Battle of Actium. He then assumed the position of emperor and became known as Augustus, the Divine (the imperial myth had him being conceived by the gods). Augustus ushered Rome into a great era of peace and stability. He was proclaimed throughout the land—on coins, inscriptions, and temples—as "Son of God," "Savior of the world," "Lord of the whole world," and "God made manifest," among other titles.

Undoubtedly, Luke is drawing a contrast between the one who would occupy the throne of David (1:32), and the one who brought peace to Rome. The peace ushered in by Augustus was a temporary peace, enforced and supported by imperial might that violently subdued all opposition. It was a kingdom maintained by violent power, exercised by the powerful.

How different is the kingdom of the Christ child! He was born, not in pomp and pageantry, but in a humble peasant's house among the animals. He did not walk among royalty in palace halls, but among the poor, oppressed, diseased, and demonized in the towns and villages of Galilee and Judea. Lowly Jewish shepherds, often despised among their own people, came to honor him, for to them and their kind he had come, bringing hope of a new world where the power of love would take the place of violent force. He did not wield sword or spear and he admonished his followers to love their enemies and pray for those who abuse them. He taught his disciples a nonviolent strategy for asserting their humanity and dignity as children of God under the crushing hands of imperial force. He pronounced blessing on peacemakers, judgment on warmongers, and he challenged all security systems rooted in wealth and control. He is a different kind of king, the viceroy of God's peaceable kingdom, and he manifested in his life, words, and deeds the character of a forgiven, healed, and restored world.

One interpreter defines the peace announced by the heavenly hosts as "that wholeness of life which God grants to persons and societies through a restoring of balance in all the forces of creation which influence our lives."[3] The classic Hebrew prophets often spoke of the restoration and renewal of Israel, but sometimes, their vision went beyond Israel to include all people and all elements of creation. In the day of God's peaceable kingdom, "nation shall not lift up sword against nation, neither shall they learn war anymore"

3. Craddock, *Luke*, 36.

(Isa 2:4). Healing and wholeness will extend to all creation, "The wolf shall live with the lamb, the leopard shall lie down with the kid . . . They will not hurt or destroy on all my holy mountain; for the earth will be full of the knowledge of the Lord as the waters cover the sea" (Isa 11:6–9).

The NRSV translates the announcement of peace to the shepherds, "and on earth peace among those whom he favors!" In keeping, however, with Luke's universal emphasis throughout his Gospel and the emphasis in 2:10 that the good news is "for all the people," it is best to translate the statement in 2:14, "on earth peace among all humankind, on whom God's favor rests." God's favor resides with all people, for to all people a Savior has been given.

We are living in a shrinking world where we are confronted, more so now than in any other period of history, with the challenge of living and working together with people of diverse religious, social, and cultural identities. Now, more than ever, we need prophets to rise up, preaching an inclusive, universal gospel, courageously declaring God's favor to be upon all people. For many Christians this will involve a reimagining of God. *Before there can be peace among people of diverse religious faiths, we may need to have our peace disturbed and our small, narrow perceptions of God challenged.* Consider the following story adapted from David Dark's book, *The Sacredness of Questioning Everything*:[4]

Imagine a tight-knit community where people share joys, sufferings, concerns, and gossip. An outsider to this community, listening in on their conversations and observing their life together, would pick up rather quickly on their

4. Dark, *The Sacredness of Questioning Everything*, 9–11.

references and allusions to "Uncle George," who seems to bind the community together.

Uncle George appears to be lurking behind all their interactions. A beautiful sunset prompts one community member to exclaim, "Isn't Uncle George awesome?" Good news and celebrative events inspire feelings of gratitude toward Uncle George. Even in tragedy, the community turns toward Uncle George for help.

At the beginning of each week the community assembles at the Community Center. There is animated conversation and fellowship as they discuss the past week's events and upcoming plans for the week ahead. When a bell sounds, the conversation ceases. Everyone descends down a stairway into the basement where a giant man in dark clothes stands with his back turned toward them, facing an enormous furnace.

When all are assembled he turns around. His look is stern and somber. His voice deep, he says, "Am I good?" They all respond in unison, "Yes, Uncle George, you are good." He then asks, "Am I worthy of praise?" "Yes," they all proclaim. "Do you love me more than anyone or anything else?" "We love you and you alone," they reply.

His face is contorted and in a frightening voice he thunders, "You better love me or I'm going to put you . . . in here!" He opens the furnace door to reveal a gaping darkness. Out of the darkness can be heard cries of anguish and misery. Then he closes the door as they sit in silence.

After a time of reflection on what they just heard, they leave and return to their life together in community. They talk about the wonders of Uncle George and they speak of his love for them as they live their lives the best they can.

But while they mention Uncle George's love, there is beneath all the talk and interaction an underlying fear and confusion—sometimes conscious, sometimes repressed, but always present. This inner fear limits their relationships, preventing them from talking about their doubts and questions, and keeping them from expressing to one another their inner anguish and uncertainties. It diminishes their lives in myriads of ways.

Sound familiar? Sometimes it is necessary "to lose one's religion" in the process of developing a healthier spirituality. *Reconstruction presumes some form of deconstruction.* Our unhealthy, fearful images of God will need to be relinquished in order to cultivate and grow a more transformational faith that drives out fear and inspires real love of God and neighbor. *As our world seems to grow smaller, our God must become larger,* a God big enough to embrace all people without restricting them to a single way of believing or threatening them with divine wrath.

If our Christianity does not move us beyond our particular Christian group, church, denomination, faith system, or doctrine to accept those who believe and practice a different faith than ours or no faith at all, then our faith will most likely be more detrimental than beneficial to the work of the kingdom of God on earth. If we cannot embrace others as God's children without requiring them to adhere to our faith system, then we will become obstacles and barriers to the creation of God's beloved community.

Our Christian faith should be a resource that compels us to hold our beliefs in humility, to work for peace, to listen to and treat others of different faith traditions with respect, and to look for common ground on which we can stand together as children of God and work for the betterment of humanity and our planet. Jesus said, "Blessed are the peacemakers, for they will be called children of God" (Matt 5:9).

Isn't it ironic and sad that so many versions of Christianity today have the opposite impact and effect, causing division and imposing rigid boundaries that separate the insiders from the outsiders? Instead of breaking down walls, creating mutual trust and building friendships, some Christians, who press others to conform and convert to their faith system, dismiss and condemn those who refuse to adopt their Christian interpretations. Until we can accept and affirm those of a different faith tradition (or no faith tradition) as children of God, it is unlikely that we will have the will and means to secure peace in our world.

I received an email once from someone who identified himself or herself as "O1T"—meaning "only one truth." More than likely, this person not only believed that there is only one truth, but that their church or Christian group alone possessed the one truth. People holding exclusive versions of the Christian faith have a tendency to insist aggressively on a single version of truth—their version.

There can be no beloved community until we recognize that every person is a child of God, whatever may be one's faith, religious affiliation, ethnic origin, culture, social state, or mental and physical condition. Each person is a child of God, precious and loved, and God's Spirit resides in every person.

Adolfo Perez Esquivel, recipient of the Nobel Peace Prize, was imprisoned by the military dictatorship of Argentina and spent eighteen months in solitary confinement. As one would expect, he went through periods of depression and experienced feelings of outrage; but ultimately, he decided that if set free, he would not seek revenge, but would work to bring in a new order where people could live in peace and dignity, and where life would be deemed sacred.

In the months after his release he struggled to live up to this vision. The words of Jesus from the cross kept haunting him, "Father, forgive them, for they know not what they do." These words made no sense to him; surely, he reasoned, they knew exactly what they were doing. But then it dawned on him. What did his torturers and oppressors not know? They did not realize they had imprisoned and were mistreating a brother, not an enemy. They were all children of God and the only way he could communicate this reality would be to forgive them and pursue a course for peace.

Until we can accept that God's unconditional love transcends all religion and belief systems and find constructive ways to embody this love, it is not likely that we will make progress creating a world of justice and peace, grounded in mutual trust and friendship.

This does not mean that diverse religious faiths are all somehow the same. There are profound differences in worldviews and beliefs among religions that cannot be harmonized. This is true, also, of different strands of tradition within a general religious perspective. For example, within Christianity there are significant differences of belief and perspective from the far right to the far left, and the same is true of other religious traditions as well. Christians who believe in an inclusive gospel acknowledge these differences, but contend that there is something deeper and truer about human beings than the differences of belief that separate us, namely, we are all children of God who, in some way, bear God's image.

No one has a monopoly on God. None of our many definitions, creeds, and belief statements comes close to capturing the actuality of Divine Reality. God is always "more,"—much more! So whenever we talk about God, we always reflect our flawed, limited understanding of God. What we think and say about God is simply the outer shell that encases the hidden pearl of what really "IS." All our beliefs are like fingers pointing to the moon. Certainly as truth-seeking Christians we strive for a reliable, healthy, and trustworthy understanding of God. We engage in theological reflection grounded in reason, common sense, the sacred Christian traditions of the past and present, and the historical-critical study of the Scriptures, and in conjunction with critical thought, we pursue a vibrant, transformative spirituality. But we never fully escape our human flaws, limitations, and biases. Any one who speaks about God should do so with great humility, realizing that anything one says is tentative and subjective.

The story in the Hebrew Bible about the priest who was struck dead for reaching out to steady the Ark of the Covenant on its trip back to Jerusalem (after it had resided with the Philistines for a time) may be a story about the folly of trying to manage God (2 Sam 6). God cannot be captured in a box, no matter how sacred or special.

We who embrace an inclusive gospel do not need to shout or defend the truth. We do not claim to be in sole possession of the truth or that our way of knowing and serving God is the only way available to humanity. We are willing to turn the questions others have onto ourselves and our faith system. Doubt is treated as an ally in the spiritual life, not an enemy. We are so grateful for the abundance of life that we have discovered in our commitment to the way of Jesus that we want to invite others to join us on the journey. We see no need, however, to push others who have no interest.

By contrast, those committed to more dualistic versions of Christianity tend to be more confrontational, and often see themselves as guardians and emissaries of the one, true way to God. They may quote Bible passages like John 14:6 and Acts 4:12, interpreting them in an exclusive way. Many believe that their view of Christian faith is the only way to find acceptance/salvation with God, so they feel a responsibility to convert others to their faith system.

Christians who take this approach rarely agree among themselves exactly what one must believe about Jesus in order to be saved. Some approaches are extremely restrictive and condemnatory, even to the point of rejecting other Christians as children of God because they do not conform to their view about the Bible, Jesus' divinity, Jesus' atoning death, or some other doctrine they think critical. One of my church members, for example, was labeled "unsaved" by a couple of his colleagues in the high school where he teaches, because they discovered that he did not believe in the virgin birth.

When we impose our "either/or" mentality onto God and make "our" way God's way, claiming that it is the "only" way, God ends up looking awfully petty and needy. Richard Rohr has pointed out in several of his writings that our flawed tendency is "not to see things as they are, but to see things as we are." We are constantly, it seems, projecting our fears and biases onto God, fashioning God in our image. This approach to Christianity, at its best, is reductionistic, pigeonholing God in our narrow belief systems; at its worst, it is arrogant, condescending, judgmental, and even deadly. An inclusive approach to the gospel does not eliminate all our biases, presuppositions, and preconceived beliefs that we bring to our understanding of God, but adherents of an inclusive gospel seem more readily to acknowledge them and refuse to be dismissive of different views and perspectives.

Religion is such a potent force in our world that the future of our planet hinges upon humankind's capacity to grow up spiritually. While it is true that we can only see a reflection of God and all our attempts to understand God fall short, we can, however, adopt an adult version of the Christian faith. We can recognize the divisiveness and destructiveness of dualistic religion and embrace a more inclusive Christianity that is compassionate, kind, credible, gracious, and affirming.[5]

Of course, it is one thing to acknowledge that we are all children of God; it's quite another to embody that reality in the way we treat one another, work together, and live together as sisters and brothers. Paul's letter to the Ephesians offers rich resources for all followers of Jesus seeking to be guided in the way of peace.[6] At the beginning of the letter, Paul states God's intention in the "fullness of time, to gather up all things" in Christ (1:10). Paul apparently believed

---

5. See my book, *The Good News According to Jesus*.

6. Some interpreters think that a disciple of Paul or someone in the Pauline tradition after Paul's death wrote Ephesians; I consider Paul to be author.

that God is in the process of drawing all things, "things in heaven and on earth," things in all realms of reality, to God's self. In this letter Paul is particularly concerned with Jew and non-Jew living in harmony as sisters and brothers in Christ. He argues that because of the self-giving of Christ in death and through corporate participation "in him," Christ has become "our peace"; he "has made both groups into one and has broken down the dividing wall, that is, the hostility" between them (Eph 2:14). Living out this reality in the daily grind of life, however, is no simple matter.

Beginning in chapter 4 Paul offered practical instructions on how to live out their unity in the midst of their diversity. And as we would expect, the call to love pervades this part of the letter,

> I therefore, the prisoner in the Lord, beg you to lead a life worthy of the calling to which you have been called, with all humility and gentleness, with patience, *bearing with one another in love*, making every effort to maintain the unity of the Spirit in the bond of peace. (4:1–3)

> But *speaking the truth in love*, we must grow up in every way into him who is the head, into Christ, from whom the whole body, joined and knit together . . . as each part is working properly, promotes the body's growth in *building itself up in love*. (4:15–16)

> Therefore, be imitators of God, as beloved children, and *live in love*, as Christ loved us and gave himself up for us, a fragrant offering and sacrifice to God. (5:1–2)

Paul speaks about the necessity of putting off anger, deception, bitterness, slander, malice, and all those destructive patterns associated with the old/false self that ignite alienation, estrangement, and enmity between persons and groups (4:25–31). He admonishes them to clothe themselves in healthy, positive virtues, to "be kind to one another, tenderhearted, forgiving one another, as God in Christ has forgiven" them (4:32).

Forgiveness, which was so central in the teachings of Jesus, is foundational to living a flourishing life in God's kingdom. There can be no reconciliation, no beloved community, no building up the body in love without forgiveness. *Forgiveness is the air we breathe in God's new world* and constitutes the soil in which the soul, as well as the whole community, grows and thrives. This is why forgiveness is at the very heart of the prayer Jesus taught his disciples to pray, "Forgive us our trespasses, as we forgive those who have trespassed against us."

Theologian Walter Wink tells about two peacemakers who visited a group of Polish Christians ten years after the end of World War II. The peacemakers asked, "Would you be willing to meet with other Christians from West Germany? They want to ask forgiveness for what Germany did to Poland during the war and begin to build a new relationship." At first there was silence. Then someone spoke up, "What you are asking is impossible. Each stone of Warsaw is soaked in Polish blood! We cannot forgive." Before they parted they said the Lord's Prayer together. They came to the part about forgiveness and everyone stopped praying. Tension welled up in the room. The one who was outspoken said, "I must say 'yes' to you or I could no longer call myself a Christian and pray to the Father. And I must tell you that humanly speaking, I cannot do it, but God will give us strength." Eighteen months later the Polish and West German Christians met together in Vienna restoring relationships.[7]

It is true that we cannot do this on our own. It is our human nature to want vengeance, to make the perpetrator of the hurt and harm done to us pay for the offense.

Forgiveness involves more than a single act or step; rather, it is a process we must work through.

Jean Vanier, founder of L'Arche, an international network of communities for people with developmental disabilities, tells about being in Rwanda shortly after the genocide. A young woman shared with him that seventy-five members of her family had been assassinated. She said, "I have so much anger and hate within me and I don't know what to do with it. Everybody is talking about reconciliation, but nobody has asked for forgiveness. I just don't know what to do with all the hate that is within me." The problem for her, says Vanier, was that she was feeling guilty for the hate she had in her heart. He said to her, "Do you know that the first step towards forgiveness is 'no vengeance'? Do you want to kill those who killed members of your family?" She said she didn't. "Well," said Vanier, "that is the first step in the process of forgiveness. No retaliation is the first step."[8]

Forgiveness is a journey, a pilgrimage, not simply an event. We grow into it. We will certainly need the support and prayers of our Christian community and we may need the professional help of a trained counselor or spiritual di-

7. Wink, *Engaging the Powers*, 275–76.
8. Vanier, *Encountering the Other*, 57.

rector. Ultimately, whether we recognize the Divine Spirit or not, forgiveness is the work of God in our souls. The living Christ galvanizes our hearts into action.

Not long ago when I accelerated to about seventy miles per hour, my car started to shake and vibrate. It needed a wheel alignment and balance. Being mechanically challenged, I know very little about this process, but my mechanic was able to make it whole again. This is what Christ can do in our personal lives and our relationships. Jesus, in John's Gospel, said to his disciples, "Peace I leave with you; my peace I give you. I do not give to you as the world gives. Do not let your hearts be troubled, and do not let them be afraid" (14:27). The gift of peace that Jesus lavishes on his disciples is *a life in balance, in proper alignment, in harmony and friendly cooperation with God, with others, and with creation.* It is the kind of peace that grows deep into the soul, influencing how we see our world and how we relate and interact with one another. It inspires inner fortitude and courage, and nurtures a calm confidence that expels fear and worry.

I mentioned at the beginning of this chapter that our relationships, interactions, and connections with others and our world cannot be separated from the inner state and condition of our souls. If we are estranged from a friend or family member, a work associate, or a casual acquaintance, then this will negatively impact our sense of self and disturb our inner peace. In certain cases, however, where persons are sociopathic or extremely narcissistic, or where there is some mental disorder or neurosis, these persons might find some sadistic pleasure or satisfaction by inflicting harm on others. Also, there may be times when we allow our anger and bitterness to fester until we find a measure of release through some means of retaliation. But these feelings and actions are the result of a deluded and severely twisted false self.

I believe that part of what we call—in theological and biblical language—"judgment" involves a process whereby we come to acknowledge, confess, and experience the pain and hurt that our selfish and destructive actions have caused others. For some of us, perhaps many of us, this process will not end in this life; for others, who are extremely egotistical, this process may hardly begin at all in this stage of existence. There may be so much darkness in the soul that the light of God "which enlightens everyone" (John 1:9) cannot break through. I do believe, however, that God will bring every human being through this process, leading us to genuine repentance and redemption. For some of us it may be a long, painful journey, but a journey that I believe will have a glorious ending; a journey that will ultimately result in healing, wholeness, and reconciliation with God, those whom we have hurt, and with all creation. I envision, in God's new creation, the victim and victimizer being redeemed and reconciled.

Peace, in all its varied expressions, is God's gift to the creation. Sometimes we experience a special kind of emotional and spiritual peace that the Spirit engenders within the soul. Author, pastor, and former preaching professor, John Killinger, tells about being in Brooklyn Heights some years ago visiting the church where Henry Ward Beecher, the famous Congregationalist minister, once preached. That evening he walked with his hostess along the promenade that overlooks Manhattan. It was a wonderful place to see Manhattan, remarked Killinger, with the ships coming in and out, and the great panorama of lights against the nighttime sky.

His hostess talked about her life when she had arrived there several years before. Her husband had left her, and she was having difficulties with her only child, a daughter. She had come to this place at night thinking she could not go on in the pain and agony she was feeling. She sat on one of the benches there and looked across the bay. She stared out at Liberty Island in the distance and she watched the tug boats as they moved in and out of the bay. She sat for a long time. The longer she sat the more her life seemed to come together and was invested with a kind of quietness that came over her spirit.

Deep down she began to feel peaceful. She told Killinger that she felt somehow that God was very near to her, as if she could reach out and touch God. Better yet, she felt that God was reaching out to her, touching her. She felt whole and complete and healed as she sat there that evening, and it became a turning point in her life.[9]

This is the work of God's Spirit in our deepest self. Paul spoke of this kind of peace in his letter to the Philippians,

> Rejoice in the Lord always; again I will say, Rejoice. Let your gentleness be known to everyone. The Lord is near. Do not worry about anything, but in everything by prayer and supplication with thanksgiving let your requests be made known to God. And the peace of God, which surpasses all understanding, will guard your hearts and your minds in Christ Jesus. (Phil 4:4–7)

---

9. Killinger, "Finding God in a Busy World, 132.

We are to do *what we can do*. We can strive, as much as possible, to maintain a positive, grateful, and hopeful attitude in the midst of our difficulties, trusting that the Lord is near. Instead of reacting harshly in an overbearing way to difficult people, we can foster a kind of gentle, but firm endurance and forbearance of one another. We can refuse to hang our heads in despair or drench our souls in worry, and we can bring to God the cries and anguish of our hearts, trusting that God's grace will be sufficient. Ultimately, though, we receive Gods peace as a gift. The peace that stands watchful guard over our minds and hearts, keeping nervous fear and anxiety at bay, is, after all, the peace "of God." God is the ultimate source that brings our lives into harmony and balance. We cannot willfully manufacture this peace in our minds and hearts, but we can create space for God to work as we entrust our lives each moment to God's provision and grace.

The way of Christ is the way of peace—with God, with our sisters and brothers in the human family, with all creation, and within our own minds and hearts. May we find the faith and courage to pursue the way of peace in route to a world reconciled and made whole.

5

The Heart of the Universe

. . . Shimmers of Divine Love

God's love was revealed among us in this way: God sent his only Son into the world so that we might live through him.

—1 John 4:9

WILLA CATHER's Christmas story, *The Burglar's Christmas*, portrays a young man named William, the proverbial prodigal son, who had moved away from his family back east and was now in Chicago. Impoverished, having been without food for several days, William decides on Christmas Eve to break into a house and steal some food. He had never stolen before, but it's Christmas Eve, he's hungry, and he thinks at least he deserves some food. When he breaks into the home, he discovers that he has burglarized the house of his parents, who had moved to Chicago. His mother catches him while stealing, and he confesses everything.

In so many words she begs him to stay, "Tonight you have come back to me, just as you always did after you ran away to swim in the river that was forbidden you, the river you loved because it was forbidden. You are tired and sleepy, just as you used to be then . . . I never asked you where you had been then, nor will I now. You have come back to me, that's all in all to me." He looks up at her questioningly and says, "I wonder if you know how much you pardon?" She responds, "O, my poor boy, much or little, what does it matter? Have you wandered so far and paid such a bitter price for knowledge and not yet learned that love has nothing to do with pardon or forgiveness, that it only loves, and loves—and loves?"[1]

The God who has come to us in Christ, "only loves, and loves—and loves." *God is continually at work in non-coercive, creative ways, revealing to us the width and depth of unconditional divine love.*

The sublime generosity and magnanimous altruism of God's love is often missed and even muddled by those of us who claim to speak for God. We would expect this to happen in the push and shove world of competitive economics and in the political maneuvering and power plays of big business and government. But much too often our religious traditions dilute and distort God's love. When religion is at its best, our sacred texts and traditions will woo and draw us into the unconditional embrace and transformative power of divine goodness. Unfortunately, however, the best of our traditions can easily get lost underneath layers of interpretation and pious practice that serve to encase God's love in dogmatic, doctrinal declarations and rigid, unalterable religious structures.

---

1. Cather, "The Burglar's Christmas," para. 60, 62–63.

The Rev Peter Gomes observes that the inclusive gospel of Jesus can easily get lost in the Bible. The Bible, says Gomes, has often been used as a blunt instrument to exclude those whose differences make us uncomfortable. Biblical standards are proclaimed that "support the status quo privileges of conventional wisdom, making the Bible a tool of oppression, the church an exclusive fellowship of shared prejudice, and the glad tidings—the gospel that Jesus came to proclaim—a mockery."[2] But Jesus, says Gomes, discovered in the Hebrew Bible, the means to the gospel. Jesus drew from the best of his Jewish tradition in order to proclaim and embody a forgiveness and love that has no limits.

God cannot dwell in a narrow heart. *Every heart that God invades and penetrates expands.* God's love courageously moves us beyond our biases and personal likes and dislikes, constantly pushing the edges and extending the boundaries. The Christian spiritual writer, Evelyn Underhill, says, "It is one of the holy miracles of love that once fairly started on that path of dedication, it cannot stop. It spreads and spreads in ever-widening circles until it embraces the whole world in God. If we begin by loving our nearest, we shall end by loving those who seemed furthest."[3]

Fr Richard Rohr shares a fascinating story he learned from a seasoned African missionary. When the priest first arrived in an African village he began by celebrating the Eucharist in a simple manner. He said to the people, "Now I'm going to celebrate a very simple means of sharing God's love with you. Those of you who want to join in this meal

2. Gomes, *The Scandalous Gospel of Jesus*, 204.
3. Underhill, *The Ways of the Spirit*, 63.

are entering into God's love." Then he held out the bread to them and said, "Whoever eats this bread believes that your people are one people." He explained to them the implication of this simple gospel, "That means you can't hate one another anymore."

Unknowingly, the priest had violated a custom of the tribe; namely, the men ate together, while the women and children ate separately. It was a disgrace for a man to eat with a woman. Unwittingly, the priest had gathered men and women around the sacred table and fed the bread to men and women as equals. This disturbed them, and the natives reacted quite vocally. The priest raised his voice over the murmurings and said, "In Christ there is no distinction between male and female."

The people were dumbfounded at that statement. They wanted to know who this Christ was who made no distinction between men and women. The priest tried to explain, "He is the father of all. That means you are all brothers and sisters, and when you eat this bread, you are one in Christ." At this, some began to move away, because it was humiliating for men to eat with women.

The great challenge for the priest was to communicate the gospel in their cultural context. For the priest the Eucharist was the essence of the gospel, so his approach was to invite them to the sacred meal and as simply as possible explain to them, day after day, the meaning and implication of the ritual. In fifteen years, this created something of a social revolution in the tribe.

One day, the men came and literally laid their weapons at his feet, saying to him, "If the gospel you preach to us is true, if this Jesus, this Son of the Father, loves us in this total way, and if he is the Father of all the people in our village and the Father of the people in the village down the road, then we can't kill them anymore." In fifteen years this tribe learned what Western Civilization hasn't been able to learn in two thousand years with all its complex versions of Christianity.

The missionary told Fr Rohr that he saw no point in confusing these people by telling them about all the different denominations in Christendom. He just wanted to communicate Jesus' and the Father's love to them. After fifteen years, there were over ten thousand practicing Christians who were celebrating the Eucharist.

Then, a bishop of Rome assigned to investigate the situation asked the priest, "Do these people know that they are Catholics?" The priest responded, "No, I haven't told them that yet." The bishop tightened up and announced that the situation was entirely out of control. He insisted that they had to know they were Catholic. The priest replied, "They are a catholic people. They are a universal people, open to all that God is saying and doing." The bishop threw up his hands and returned to Rome.

The priest started thinking about how upset the bishop was and that perhaps he should teach them about the seven sacraments. So he gathered some of the elders together and explained to them that a sacrament is an encounter between God and humans, and that there were seven of these. All the elders looked puzzled, and finally one of them said, "But we thought there were at least seven hundred!"

It was at that moment the priest realized that he would be limiting their perception of Divine Reality if he were to insist that there were only seven moments when God encounters humans. These people were already sacramentally minded and more incarnational than even the most devout Westerners. They had no problem thinking that God communicates with humans through signs, symbols, rituals, and gestures; their whole lives were filled with these things. They couldn't imagine limiting these to seven.[4]

Such is the beauty, power, simplicity, and universality of an inclusive gospel. Are we better off with our sophisticated religious systems? With our complex doctrinal formulations, absolute truth claims, literalistic interpretations, and exclusive religious practices, we often reduce, restrict, and retard the redemptive and transformative power of God's universal, unconditional love.

Some versions of Christianity teach and imagine God in ways that strike fear in the hearts of worshippers. But we have no reason to be afraid of God. God's love drives out fear. Not all fear is bad, however. Fear, in its essence—at its most basic level—is a reaction to a threat, and is a common human instinct. At times fear can prove useful.

A man who worked the four to midnight shift walked home every night past a cemetery. One night, in a hurry, he decided to take a shortcut through the cemetery. The route lopped five minutes off his walk, and soon it became his regular path. But on one particularly dark night, he had the unfortunate mishap of falling into a freshly dug grave. He wasn't hurt, but the hole was so deep he was unable to get out. He yelled for help but nobody heard him. He tried his best to climb up the side, but to no avail. Finally, he resigned himself to simply wait for morning, when his plight would be discovered. He pulled his coat up around his neck and

4. Rohr, *The Good News According to Luke*, 44–46.

huddled in a corner of the hole to try to sleep. He was able to doze off, but then he was suddenly awakened in an hour or so by the noise of a falling body. A second unfortunate man had stumbled into the same grave. Sleepily, the first arrival watched as his companion first screamed for help, and then frantically tried to crawl out. After a few minutes he felt obliged to comment, "Hey buddy, you will never get out that way." Well—he did!

Fear can be a motivating factor and it may supply the help and empowerment we need for a temporary fix in certain situations, but fear will not grow the soul nor change one's basic nature. It provides a fragile foundation for real soul development and personal or communal transformation. As described in 1 John, "There is no fear in love, but perfect [mature] love casts out fear; for fear has to do with punishment, and whoever fears has not reached perfection [maturity] in love" (1 John 4:18). *Great experiences of love, not fear, empower transformation.*

One of the common teachings of Johannine Christianity reiterated throughout 1 John is that love for God is inseparably linked to love for one another (1 John 3:16–18; 4:7–8, 12, 19–21). If we cannot love our brothers and sisters in the human family, then we cannot love God, and the love of God does not dwell in us. Jesus made this point when he connected love for God with love for neighbor as the sum and substance of true religion.

Our love for one another, and hence, our love for God, is demonstrated through concrete, specific acts of kindness, forgiveness, generosity, and grace (1 John 3:16–18). We share out of our time and resources to encourage and build up others. Our commitment to God is expressed in our commitment to one another. As the writer of 1 John observes, "Those who abide in love abide in God, and God abides in them" (4:16b).

As we grow in our love for one another, we will grow in our love for God. Once there was a young Jewish man who went to his rabbi and confessed that he didn't know how to love God. He asked the rabbi if he would teach him how to love God. The rabbi said, "Find a stone. Try to love the stone. Try to see its beauty and let it come into you. Then when you can love a stone, try a flower. See if you can let its beauty and goodness soak into your soul. Don't pluck it or possess it. Just love it in its natural setting." The rabbi knew the young man had a dog and so he said, "Then make sure you love your dog and care for your dog. And when you have loved your dog, next try to love the sky and the mountains. Be present to them in their many forms. Let them speak to you and come into you. Then," said the rabbi, "try to love a woman. Be faithful to a woman and sacrifice for her. After you have loved a stone, a flower, your dog, the mountains and the sky, and a woman, then you'll be ready to love God."

As we learn to love the creation and become good stewards of God's world, and as we learn how to love, care for, and be faithful to one another, then we will learn how to love God. If a person does not know how to love the things of the earth, or how to love his or her sisters and brothers in the human (God's) family, then that person will not know how to love God. The writer of 1 John says, "Those who do not love a brother or sister whom they have seen, cannot love God whom they have not seen" (4:20b). There are traces of God in every person.

The writer of 1 John declares that as we learn to love one another, God's love is perfected in us (4:12); that is, God's love is formed in us in such a way that we become well-developed and mature in God's love. This is no sentimental kind of love. Loving others demands that we attend to others mentally, emotionally, and with our whole personalities. *Since God indwells every person, when we spontaneously and intentionally give ourselves to others, we are giving ourselves to God and entering into God's very life.* As we become more aware of and sensitive to God's love, we become more skillful and wise in the ways we express love to others. Love for God and love for the world forms a never-ending loop.

According to the writer of 1 John, God sent Jesus to reveal to us the extent of God's love and to teach us how to love. The biblical writer says, "In this is love, not that we loved God but that he loved us and sent his Son to be the atoning sacrifice for our sins" (1 John 4:10). Jesus' death was the culmination of a life given to sacrificial service and self-giving for the good of others. As such, it demonstrates powerfully the depth of God's love for the world.

The movie *Out of Africa* is an early twentieth century story of a Danish woman who leaves her country to purchase and operate a large coffee plantation in Kenya. One evening she wakes and the plantation is ablaze. The sacks of coffee and the machines that process the coffee beans are on fire. She watches helplessly as everything is lost. She has no way of rebuilding and must leave the country. Before she leaves, she is determined to find land for the natives who once worked for her.

Shortly before her scheduled departure, she attends a party for the new governor of Kenya. The governor takes her hand and says, "Baroness, I'm sorry to hear that Kenya will be losing you." She says, "You have heard my trouble then?" He responds, "Yes, I regret it." She then inquires, "And do you know of my problem now?" The aides attempt to interrupt her, but the governor says, "This land you want from us?" She implores, "Will you help me, Sir Joseph?" The governor is hesitant, "That's quite difficult."

Suddenly the baroness gets down on her knees, while the political entourage protests. The governor orders, "Get up, Baroness, please!" as guests begin to stare. The baroness remains on her knees. She says, "Kenya is a hard country for women. So there is a chivalry here, of a sort. You are a powerful man, and I have no one else to turn to. You mustn't be embarrassed. I've lost everything. It costs me very little to beg you. This land is theirs, you see. We took it. And now they've nowhere else to go."

The governor says, "I'll look into it. We'll do the best we can." He holds out his hand. She takes his hand and asks, "May I have your word, sir?" The governor again hedges. But just then the governor's wife stands up and says, "You have mine." The women shake hands, and she is escorted from the room.[5]

The love of God that finds unique, visible expression in the incarnation of Christ *is not only humble, it is willing to endure humiliation*, all the way to a Roman cross. God's love, however, is not soft or weak. I am reminded of the woman who was doing some last-minute Christmas shopping at an over-crowded mall and was quite frustrated.

5. *Out of Africa*, Universal Pictures, 1985.

With her arms full of packages, she pushed her way into an elevator that was already packed. Finally inside, she blurted out, "Whoever is responsible for this whole Christmas thing ought to be shot." From somewhere in the elevator a voice exclaimed, "Don't worry, lady, they already crucified him."

Jesus, empowered by divine love, challenged the powers that be and stood in solidarity with the poor, oppressed, marginalized, and excluded, confronting the gatekeepers of conventional religion and the powerbrokers of the social order. Courageously, he preached, taught, and lived the kingdom of God, and the kingdoms of the world were offended and outraged. In our discipleship to Jesus we are called to love like him.

Too often, however, the church has been reluctant to incarnate Jesus' passion for the poor and to share sacrificially in his ministry to set the oppressed free. Dr. Fred Craddock tells about the time he was teaching homiletics and New Testament at a small school in Oklahoma. The school was hanging on by its financial fingernails. The president of the school said to Fred, "I'm in touch with a man who is concerned about improving the quality of preaching in Oklahoma. He has a lot of money and I believe he's going to give a sizable gift to our preaching program. Will you go with me to talk to him?"

Fred was delighted to go, so he and the president went to visit the man at his office. He was waiting for them and ready to hand over the gift. He said, "Before we finish this I think we ought to pray." Neither Fred nor the president prayed. The man prayed. He had the money and he had the prayer. With pen in hand, he was about to sign the check. His lawyer had everything prepared. This was a large donation. But before he signed, he looked up and said, "Now, this all goes for the preaching program?" They said, "Yes sir, that's what it goes for." He started to write, but paused again and said, "Now, you do understand, none of this goes for women or for blacks."

The president stood up. Fred stood up. The president said, "I'm sorry, we cannot accept your money under those conditions." As they started to leave the man spoke up, "Well, there are plenty of schools that will." And he was right. That man had given over sixty million dollars to schools and churches, but not a penny to women or African-Americans.[6]

When we abide in God's love and stand in solidarity with the marginalized, *there will be times when we have to swim against the swift current of popular opinion, common cultural values and standards, and corrupt corporate practices, even at the risk of drowning.* Those who are compelled by divine love are not only committed to comfort and encourage the hurting, they are also willing, at great personal sacrifice, to challenge and confront the powers that be who are determined to muzzle and immobilize any opposing voice.

Loving like Jesus is easier to talk about than to do. I heard about an unmarried man who traveled all around the country giving a lecture on "Ten Commandments for Parents." Then he fell in love and got married. After the arrival of his first baby, he changed his talk to "Ten Suggestions for Parents." With the coming of the second baby his talked was called, "Ten Helpful Hints for Parents." When a third child came, he stopped giving the talk altogether. It can be

6. Craddock, *Craddock Stories*, 141.

difficult practicing and living the principles we like to talk about.

God's love is the energy of the universe. When this energy pulsates through our thoughts, attitudes, and actions, and vibrates through our conversation and conduct, then our spirits are electrified with the joy, mystery, wonder, and sheer gift of life. *As we become conductors through whom God's love flows, we become God's gift to others who need fresh experiences of God's grace and goodness.* As the current of divine love arcs outward into the lives of the people we touch, we serve as mediators of the light and radiance of the divine presence.

One of my favorite Christmas stories is about a little church that traditionally had a Christmas play for all the children and the "adult children" who loved it just as much. There was a ten-year old boy named Barry who had been a disaster in every Christmas play in which he had been involved. One year his angel wings caught on fire, which nearly burned down the church. The next year, as Herod the Great, he jumped from his throne and, in his usual clumsy way, jerked the carpet out from under the three wise men and dumped them on their heads.

The children begged the director not to let Barry ruin another Christmas play, "Please, teacher, could you leave Barry out this year?"

But how could she reject a little boy who tried his best and loved Jesus with all his heart, even if he was a bit clumsy? She was able to convince the other children that Barry couldn't do any real damage by playing the innkeeper of Bethlehem. He just opened and closed a door and spoke one short line. What damage could he possibly do?

The Heart of the Universe

Barry made it through all the rehearsals and the dress rehearsal perfectly. Then, the big night arrived, when all the mothers, fathers, grandmothers, grandfathers, friends, and loved ones gathered to relive the Christmas story with their children. Barry was given a chance to redeem himself from all his previous mishaps. He opened the door of the inn and looked straight into the face of Mary and Joseph. Mary, very sad and pale, sat on a little donkey, which they had never used in practice. The scene looked so real.

On that special night when all the props were in place and with Mary playing her part so well, you could almost hear the wind whistling around the cold stone walls of the inn and blowing the thin cloak of gentle Mary. When it was Barry's time to speak, he spoke out loudly and clearly. His timing and emphasis were impeccable, "Be gone, I have no room for the likes of you!" Then Barry watched Mary and Joseph turn sadly away into the cold night. Those on the front row later said that they saw tears well up in Barry's eyes and his lips start to tremble.

"Wait!" cried Barry. It came like a thunderclap. Every heart in the room stopped! This wasn't in the script of the familiar Christmas story.

Then Barry finished it, "Wait! You can have my room!" All bedlam broke loose. The children cried, the parents roared, and pandemonium reigned. Barry had done it again; he had ruined another Christmas play. But then, maybe not.

The director quieted the crowd and said, "Maybe, just maybe, Barry has given us the greatest message of all. He could not turn away the Christ child, even in a play."

What about us? Will we shut Jesus out? When we turn away from a world in need, from the cries of creation for mending and healing, from our brothers and sisters who are lonely, oppressed, wounded, and lost, we turn away from Christ. When we offer food to the hungry, water to the thirsty, clothes to the destitute, and companionship to the lonely, we are offering these things to Christ (Matt 24:34–40).

I read somewhere that during the filming of *The Misfits*, Arthur Miller, who was married to Marilyn Monroe, watched his wife descend into the depths of depression and despair. He feared for her life as he observed their growing estrangement, her paranoia, and her dependence on barbiturates. One evening while she was sleeping, after a doctor had been persuaded to give her yet another shot, Miller stood over her. Commenting on that moment he said, "I found myself straining to imagine miracles. What if she were to wake and I were able to say, 'God loves you, darling,' and she were able to believe it! How I wished I still had my religion and she hers."

Can we really believe this? Can we believe that God loves us each one with an unconditional love that drives out all fear; a love that will never give up on us and never let us go? What a difference it would make if we could. When we are confident that we are forever God's beloved children, then we are empowered to love God's creation and one another with the unconditional love of God.

6

The Love that Sent Him

. . . Shimmers of Transforming Grace

DID YOU know there are special dietary graces available only during the Christmas season? If you eat something and no one else sees it, it has no calories. If you drink a diet drink with a candy bar, the calories in the candy bar are canceled out by the diet drink. When you eat with someone else, the calories don't count if you don't eat more than they do. And all movie related foods are calorie free because they are part of the entire entertainment package, including Milk Duds, buttered popcorn, Hershey Bars, Junior Mints, and Tootsie Rolls. Wouldn't it be great if these graces could actually be appropriated?

The writer of the letter to Titus speaks of the kind of grace to which disciples of Jesus entrust their lives,

> For the grace of God has appeared, bringing salvation to all, training us to renounce impiety

> and worldly passions, and in the present age to live lives that are self-controlled, upright, and godly, while we wait for the blessed hope and the manifestation of the glory of our great God and Savior, Jesus Christ. He it is who gave himself for us that he might redeem us from all iniquity and purify himself a people of his own who are zealous of good deeds. Titus 2:11–14

The "grace of God" has been part and parcel of creation and the warp and woof of human existence from the beginning of the origin of life; but, at a definitive juncture in the evolution of humanity (or for that matter, in the evolution of the universe) the "grace of God" appeared in the person of Jesus of Nazareth. John's Gospel expresses it this way, "In the beginning was the Word . . . And the Word became flesh and lived among us, and we have seen his glory . . . full of grace and truth . . . From his fullness we have all received, grace upon grace" (John 1:1, 14, 16). Grace in exchange for grace. God's grace is inexhaustible; whenever grace is dispensed, whenever grace is lavishly outpoured, there is unlimited grace to take its place. *Like a kid with a sand bucket drawing water out of the ocean, there rests constantly before us an ocean of grace to sustain and empower human life.* Christians have become aware of the vastness of God's grace through the life, death, and resurrection of Jesus.

In declaring that Jesus Christ "gave himself for us that he might redeem us from all iniquity and purify for himself a people of his own who are zealous for good deeds" (2:14), the writer is drawing upon imagery from the Exodus,

> You have seen what I did to the Egyptians, and how I bore you on eagles' wings and brought you

> to myself. Now therefore, if you obey my voice and keep my covenant, you shall be my treasured possession out of all the peoples. Indeed, the whole earth is mine, but you shall be for me a priestly kingdom and a holy nation. Exod 19:4–6

God acted in covenant love and loyalty to the promise made to Abraham by delivering Israel from the oppression of the Egyptians. In so acting, God entered into a new arrangement with Israel, calling out Israel to be a people commissioned to make God's grace known.

All the earth is God's and all the world's people are God's children; but God set Israel apart as a special colony, a holy nation, a treasured people, a representative sample of humanity to serve as a witness to God's saving purpose for the world. God's act of deliverance called forth a new covenant relationship, a new creative partnership with Israel, leading to a new stage in God's evolving revelation of God's Self and will. And with this new arrangement came new responsibilities.

God is ever calling us forward to face new challenges, new tasks, and new responsibilities, expanding our experience, understanding, and vision of God's grace and goodness. Human history, as well as all creation, is moving somewhere; it has purpose and meaning. Jesus identified this "somewhere" as the "kingdom of God" ("kingdom of heaven" in Matthew's Gospel). Jesus undoubtedly drew from his own rich traditions, especially those of the classical Hebrew prophets, to fuel his imagination and expand his vision of God's peaceable kingdom, a world healed and made right. But Jesus also infused the phrase with fresh meaning, so that the kingdom of God functions as a dynamic, intensive symbol for the transforming, redeeming power of God currently at work in the world. When some of the religious leaders attributed his healing of the diseased and demonized to Satan, Jesus contended that he made people whole by the power of the Spirit, thus demonstrating that the transforming reality of the kingdom of God was present (Matt 12:28). *The whole-making, renewing power of the Spirit is the power of the Messianic age, and that power is presently among us and in us* (Luke 17:20–21).

A disgruntled college professor who was antagonistic toward Christianity, enjoyed provoking and frustrating his Christian students. One day as part of his presentation to his undergraduate philosophy class, he wrote on the board, "God is no where." When the professor stepped out of the classroom during the break, one of the students slipped up to the board and rearranged the letters in the sentence. He took the 'w' off the word "where" and added it to the end of the word "no," so that it read, "God is now here."

As reflected in the above passage from Titus, many of the early Christians maintained "the blessed hope" of a more complete "manifestation of the glory" of Christ in the last days, in the time of ultimate fulfillment of the Messianic kingdom, which they believed was imminently forthcoming. Many Christians, still today, entertain that hope. On the other hand, we witness the manifestation of Christ's glory every day. Christ's presence and grace can be seen and felt in the afterglow of a summer rain, the delightful smile of a little child, the embrace and friendship of loving friends and family, and in the multitude of gracious encounters, creative endeavors, and life-enhancing experiences we share with others and with creation continuously.

In the film, *Babette's Feast*, adapted from a short story by Isak Dinesen, Babette, a former *cordon bleu* chef in Paris who lost everything in the terrorist uprisings of 1871, flees to Denmark. She is taken in by two sisters who have dedicated their lives to the religious community founded by their father. Their father had long since died, and with his death the community lost its early vibrant spirit, though it maintained its puritanical strictness. Both sisters had given up the man of their dreams, along with their worldly opportunities, in order to remain in the community. Now, years later, they are weary and disillusioned as the aging community to which they had given their lives' implodes, dissolving and disintegrating in dissension and bitterness.

Babette works incognito. No one knows that she was once a famous chef. She cooks strictly in accordance with the sisters' rules and recipes, serving up a rather dull, bland regimen of food. But then, in a sudden twist of plot, Babette learns that she has won the lottery back in Paris—10,000 francs.

She offers as a gift to the community a French banquet, as a way of celebrating the birthday of the sisters' father, the community founder. The sisters dislike the idea, but they do not know how to gracefully tell her no. The community, too, is nervous about accepting this extraordinary offer. Reluctantly they decide to allow Babette to cook the meal. They vow, however, to occupy their minds with spiritual things and not to think about the food they eat, quoting Jesus, "take no thought of food and drink."

Babette has to order all the provisions from France. She spends the entire sum of her winnings bringing in a caravan of gourmet delights. When the evening of the feast arrives, at the last minute a famous vacationing general, General Lowenhielm, the man who years before had sought the hand of one of the sisters, is invited to attend. The community gathers around the table in the sisters' home as course after course of gourmet food and drink is brought in, each with its own crystal goblets, china, and flatware.

With each new drink and dish, the general is startled and amazed as he holds up a glass or dish expressing wonder and delight at its excellence. As the meal proceeds, the spirit of the group grows lighter and sweeter in spite of the vow they made not to enjoy the meal. The table talk becomes more and more congenial and free as the tensions within the group relax with each new course of food and drink. The general offers a toast that serves as the grand climax of the story,

> Man in his weakness and shortsightedness believes he must make choices in this life. He trembles at the risk he takes. We do know fear. But no. Our choice is of no importance. There comes a time when our eyes are opened. And we come to realize that mercy is infinite. We need only await it with confidence and receive it with gratitude. Mercy imposes no conditions. And, lo! Everything we have chosen has been granted to us. And everything we rejected has also been granted. Yes, we get back even what we

> rejected. For mercy and truth are met together.
> Righteousness and bliss shall kiss one another.[1]

The general's gratitude and wonderment, expressed in response to the lavish feast offered so freely by Babette, enables the community to grasp something of the breadth and depth of God's grace.

Due to the extravagant gift of God effusively poured out on us through Jesus Christ and our experience and participation in this gift, we who constitute the community of Christ followers, Christ's church, his body in the world, *must inevitably be a community of grace*—a place of welcome, hospitality, acceptance, forgiveness, generosity, and gratitude. Any Christian community that is given to quarreling and bickering, and marked by dissension and disintegration, is completely out of step with the gospel.

The writer of the letter to Titus also proclaims that God saved us according to his "goodness and loving kindness . . . not because of any works of righteousness that we had done, but according to his mercy" (Titus 3:4). He declares that the Spirit has been poured out on us richly through Jesus Christ and that we have been justified—put right with God and each other—by grace (3:6–7). No person will ever stand before God accepted on his or her own merit and worth. God takes the initiative; God works within individuals, communities, and all creation to bring healing and renewal. God's gracious, persuasive (non–coercive) power works in conjunction with our freedom to either receive or reject such power, to say "yes" or "no" to participation in the creative, regenerating grace of God at work in the world. Therefore, *all authentic*

---

1. *Babettes Feast*, Panorama Film International, 1987.

spiritual experience is rooted in humility. As one commentator observes, "Religion begins from and with humility, and without such humility it never begins at all."[2]

A mouse made her home in the wall of the university psychology laboratory. One day she decided to take her two children on a walk through the lab. On their return, they discovered a huge cat blocking their entrance. The children, of course, were terrified. The mother, however, looked the cat straight in the eye and started to bark. The cat turned tail and fled. The mother mouse said to her children, "Children, it never hurts to learn a second language." In our "survival of the fittest" culture where comparisons of worth are rendered daily in a system of competition and meritocracy, grace may seem like a second language. But in God's kingdom, it is the common form of speech. It is the sole reason we are "heirs according to the hope of eternal life" (Titus 3:7). Eternal life, life that is lived in harmony with and in collaboration with God, is available now as a pledge of what is to come in the evolving, unfolding life of God, which is intertwined and interlocked with the creation.

A relationship with God grounded in grace compels us to relinquish all claims to worldly accolades and commendations, as we stand naked before God. Here is what we need to remember: when divested of all our titles, achievements, honors, rewards, and labels, when stripped of all our talents, resources, and education, as well as all the institutions and friends that have helped us to succeed in life, *when reduced to the bare essence of who we are, vulnerable and exposed, this is the person God loves and accepts.*

---

2. Dunn, *The First and Second Letters to Timothy*, 879.

This does not mean, however, that what we do is unimportant. Our good works, while not constituting the basis for our acceptance before God, should not be denigrated or disparaged in any way. Though they do not constitute the roots of our connection with God nor the grounds for our discipleship to Christ, they certainly express the authenticity and manifest the fruit of this divine–human relationship. Good works are an indispensable, inevitable expression of our covenant relationship with God. As we fall, without props and support, into the wide arms of God's mercy, our acceptance empowers us to rise to our feet and pursue the path of righteousness, zealous of good deeds.

While we "wait for the blessed hope" of God's reign to come in fullness, for all creation to be renewed, all wrongs to be made right, and all evil judged and redeemed, we do not wait in idleness. Our present appropriation of God's salvation means personal growth, community development, and commitment to the good of the earth and humanity. By allowing God to be in charge of our lives, we enter into the "now" of God's new world. The Spirit of God, the agent and means of our "rebirth and renewal" (Titus 3:5), forms and shapes us in this present age. As Paul explains, "And all of us, with unveiled faces, seeing the glory of the Lord as though reflected in a mirror, are being transformed into the same image from one degree of glory to another; for this comes from the Lord, the Spirit" (2 Cor 3:18). This image to which we aspire and to which end the Spirit is forming us, is God's image reflected beautifully in the life and character of Jesus Christ.

The biblical writer says that grace teaches and trains us "to renounce impiety and worldly passions, and in the present age to live lives that are self-controlled, upright, and godly" (Titus 2:12). Here the writer is speaking of a disciplined life, not a rigid, legalistic life. Some folks have rather strange, distorted ideas about what constitutes an upright and godly life, or to employ a similar biblical word, a "holy" life. In a conversation with a group of male students at the Bible college I attended, I recall one gentleman telling us about how his girlfriend's hair extended down to her knees. Then he remarked, "She's so holy," making a bizarre connection between holiness and hair length.

Jesus redefined holiness for many of his contemporaries. In the holiness code, rigidly imposed on the Jewish community by the religious establishment, there were numerous laws governing all kinds of activities and behaviors. These laws, based on the Torah and oral tradition, included strict ritual washings, detailed instructions regarding Sabbath observance, and rules regulating human contact and interaction, especially pertaining to table fellowship. A dominant theme in the Gospels relates to Jesus challenging and violating these laws, bringing upon himself the wrath of the religious, social, and political powers.

The godliness/holiness that Jesus exuded and called his followers to emulate was *a godliness of compassion*. Jesus' relationship with God and immersion in God's Spirit inspired a life of compassion, a life of welcome and hospitality, and a life of trust and gratitude—the opposite of a life of austerity and rigidity that characterized hierarchical Jewish religion at the time. Jesus taught his followers to live in carefree trust in God's goodness and to be governed by love.

After Jesus was anointed by the Spirit and affirmed by the Father at his baptism, the Spirit led Jesus into the desert wilderness to face the tempter. The temptations Jesus confronted were not temptations to do evil, for any enticement toward evil would not have appealed to Jesus at all. Rather, these were temptations to do good by utilizing the means and the methods of the world. By turning stones into bread he could feed the hungry; by dazzling the crowds with spectacular feats and commanding their allegiance as the messianic king, Jesus could channel the world's resources to accomplish much good. If he would only compromise his principles, his integrity and loyalty to God, and grab the power, prominence, and position the tempter was offering him, then he could immediately put his fame and fortune to good use to save the world. It took great discipline and self-control for Jesus to say "no" to such "worldly passions."

As we draw from the wellspring of God's mercy, as we allow the creative energy of the Spirit to form us, as we follow the teachings of grace incarnate in Jesus our Lord, our passions will be gradually transformed. No longer will we be held captive by worldly passions for position, prestige, power, and possessions. No longer will we be enslaved by ego desires that spark malice, envy, and hate, catapulting us downward in a spiral of jealous bickering and contemptuous quarreling that ends in division, disintegration, and estrangement. As we wade into the ocean of God's grace and learn to swim in a sea of divine mercy, we find our identity and security in being God's special people, God's beloved children. Being confident of, joyful in, and grateful for such grace, we become eager to do what is good, to live in right relation with all God's creation, and *to become in actuality what we already are by title and name, God's beloved community.*

The biblical writer draws a stark contrast between the ego-centered life and the Spirit-controlled life (Titus 3:3-8). These scriptural contrasts between a Christian's old life ruled by the false self, and the Christian's new life formed in Christ, are no doubt overdrawn at times, but they nevertheless, in no uncertain terms, point Christ followers toward what is possible in God's new world. Being "justified"—put right with God, with our brothers and sisters in the human family, and with all creation—by grace (3:7), we live by grace, and *the grace that appeared, reappears in us.*

As we are reborn and renewed repeatedly by the Spirit, the fruit of the Spirit—the character of Christ—is produced in us: "love, joy, peace, patience, kindness, generosity, faithfulness, gentleness, and self-control" (Gal 5:22). This is true freedom, for "against such things," says Paul, "there is no law." Disciples of Jesus taught by grace and saturated with God's love, do not need rules and regulations to guide their conduct or control their conversation. Love abhors any attitude or action that seeks to manipulate, deceive, or do harm to another. Love does not insist on its own way; it is not self serving. Love bears, trusts, hopes, and endures all things for the good and growth of the other (1 Cor 13:4–7).

In Luke's infancy narrative, the angelic messenger tells Mary, "The Holy Spirit will come upon you, the power of the Most High will overshadow you; therefore the child to be born will be holy; he will be called the Son of God" (Luke 1:15). Just as the Holy Spirit came upon Mary, may it be our desire this Advent season for the Spirit of God to come upon us in ever-vibrant and fresh ways, so that the "holy" compassion and grace of the Son of God might be born in us anew.

The Love that Sent Him

Once there was an old priest who presided over a great cathedral in a once-prosperous city. The kindly priest spent his days praying in the vestry and caring for the poor. As a result of his tireless work, this holy place was known as a place of safety and sanctuary, and a constant stream of people seeking shelter were drawn to it. The priest welcomed all and gave to all completely without prejudice or restraint. His pure heart and gift of hospitality were widely known. No one could steal from him, for he considered no possession his own.

One evening in mid-winter, while the priest was praying before the cross, there was a knock on the cathedral door. The priest stood, went to the entrance, and to his great surprise, found there a terrifying demon with unyielding eyes. "Old man," the demon hissed, "I have traveled many miles to seek your shelter. Will you welcome me in?" Without hesitation, the priest bid the devil welcome and invited him into the shelter of the sanctuary. Once across the threshold, the devil spat venom onto the tiled floor and attacked the holy altar, all the while uttering blasphemies and curses. During this rant, the priest knelt on the floor and continued in his devotions until it was time for him to retire for the evening.

"Old man," cried the demon, "where are you going?" "I am returning home to rest, for it has been a long day," replied the kindly priest. "May I come with you," asked the demon, "for I too am tired and in need of a place to eat and sleep?" "Why yes, of course," replied the priest, "come, and I will prepare a meal."

On returning to his house, the priest prepared a meal while the devil smashed the artifacts that adorned the house.

He ate the meal provided by the priest and then asked, "Old man, you welcomed me into your church and then into your house. I have one more request. Will you welcome me into your soul?" "Why of course," said the priest. "What I have is yours and what I am is yours."

So the devil entered his soul, but there was nothing in the old man for the devil to cling to, no material of which to make a nest and no darkness in which to hide. All that existed in the old priest's soul was light. And so the devil turned from the priest in disgust and left, never to return. In fact, the devil, not long after his encounter with the priest, retired from his devilish work altogether, for there was something in the old man that so affected the devil that he lost his edge for it and had to give it up.

If only we could be like this priest, and be *so full of the light of love and grace that there would be no place for darkness to reside or evil to hide*. Then we would truly have the mind of Christ and could say with this priest, whose soul was full of God, "What I have is yours and what I am is yours."

What I often find in my own soul, however, is a strange paradox. My life tends to be filled with empty things. These empty things take up the space where the love of God could grow and flourish. I have to admit honestly that, all too often, my soul becomes a breeding ground for all kinds of false attachments and preoccupations. So if I want to experience God's gift of a flourishing life, I must honestly confess my attachment to desires and "worldly passions" that prevent the redeeming power of divine love from taking root. I must let go of all lesser interests and loves, so that "good soil" is available for the divine seed of love to blossom and thrive. Philosopher and theologian, Peter Rollins states that "to be a Christian is to be born of love, transformed by love and committed to transforming the world with love."[3] By allowing our souls to be a dwelling place for God, in which God can abide and out of which the divine love can flow, then "we will become the iconic spaces in which God is made manifest in the world."[4]

Mary made her womb available for a holy conception and birth. She surrendered to the mysterious, divine working of God, knowing that the holy child within her would change the world. May we, too, open our minds, hearts, and bodies to the mysterious working of God, so that the Son of God may be formed in us, and that others may see reflected in us shimmers of the divine grace that appeared in Christ, bringing salvation to all.

---

3. Rollins, *How (Not) to Speak of God*, 71.
4. Ibid., 71.

7

God with Us

. . . *Shimmers of a Deeper Joy*

But the angel said to them [the Shepherds], "Do not be afraid; for see—I am bringing you good news of great joy for all the people: to you is born this day in the city of David a Savior, who is the Messiah, the Lord."

—Luke 2:10

When Herod saw that he had been tricked by the wise men, he was infuriated, and he sent and killed all the children in and around Bethlehem who were two years old or under, according to the time that he had learned from the wise men. Then was fulfilled what had been spoken through the prophet Jeremiah: "A voice was heard in Ramah, wailing and loud lamentation, Rachel weeping for her children; she refused to be consoled, because they are no more."

—Matt 2:16–18

In the Lukan birth and infancy story there is much rejoicing, beginning with Elizabeth and Zachariah singing, prophesying, and praising God. Mary's song of praise follows. Then, the angel announces good news of great joy to the shepherds, followed by the heavenly host praising and glorifying God. Finally, Luke features Simeon and Anna in the temple, prophesying and rejoicing in God's salvation. Joy floods the narrative.

Joy is present in the Matthean narrative with the announcement that the child conceived in Mary by the Holy Spirit will save his people from their sins. This joy, however, is overshadowed and sent fleeing with the holy family's flight into Egypt and the loud cries of lamentation from the parents of the children slaughtered in Bethlehem.

The two accounts remind us that both joy and sorrow are part and parcel of the human condition. *Both exuberant delight and torturous affliction constitute the crux and context in which our salvation is worked out.*

Certainly not everyone feels like rejoicing this Christmas season. There are families dealing with difficult issues that threaten to rip them apart. Some are facing financial hardship, with little prospects of finding employment in the struggling economy. Others are grieving over the loss of loved ones, a grief that seems to intensify with the sights and sounds of Christmas. Still others are trying to find some balance after hurtful divorces and fractured relationships. Can we speak of joy for those who are ravaged by physical disease, or cut deep by bitter wounds of betrayal, or disillusioned by dashed dreams, or feel trapped by their circumstances? There will be weeping this Christmas season because the trials and tragedies of life do not take a Christmas holiday.

Church historian and theologian, Bill Leonard tells about a Christmas Eve service in Massachusetts where he was scheduled to speak. The church was packed as snow gently fell outside. Advent candles flickered off stained-glass windows in a white framed meeting house over a hundred years old. It was a picturesque Christmas scene, like one you might see on a Hallmark greeting card. As Dr. Leonard arose to deliver the message, the daughter of one of the most beloved church members experienced an unexpected seizure. Leonard thought, "Not now God. Not during my nice sermon on this beautiful Christmas Eve!" But suffering doesn't keep schedules. Their idyllic Christmas Eve service was interrupted with the need to minister to a young woman who was traumatized by physical convulsions she could not control.

Life is filled with interruptions of tumult and tribulation. For some folks, the terrible and tragic are as much a part of their daily life as eating and drinking. The abundant life made available to us in Christ does not provide immunity against the discomfort and distresses of life. *Any version of Christian faith that downplays suffering or attributes it to God's displeasure needs to reinvent itself.*

The intricacies of the interplay between divine power, divine goodness, and human freedom will always be a mystery. Jesus believed that God loves the creation and is creatively engaged in its healing and redemption. Jesus taught that God knows the number of hairs on our heads, which is to say that God takes special interest in each one of us. Even the minor players of creation, according to Jesus, do not escape God's attention, for God observes a little sparrow when it falls to the ground. Jesus' faith was firmly grounded in the goodness of God. He was convinced that God is "for" the creation.

God's care for the creation, however, does not prevent bad things from happening that are the opposite of God's good will. We live in an open universe. God has bestowed upon and built into creation the element of freedom. This freedom is essential to the biological, evolutionary processes of life. God does not (or perhaps cannot given the nature of reality) intervene to stop hurricanes and floods, nor does God alter the processes of life so that children are born free of mental disabilities and physical handicaps. This holds true in the moral life as well. We are granted the freedom to do good or evil, to harm or heal, to destroy or save life. The Herods of the world exercise their freedom to dispose of any person or group that threatens their position and power.

Freedom, then, is at the core of evolutionary life and moral existence. It is, of course, influenced and limited by many factors: genetics, time and place, circumstances of birth, education, the entire socialization process, and numerous factors beyond our control. Cancer strikes randomly, as do terrorists exercising their God–given freedom.

God does not override this freedom. God does not intervene to stop holocausts, genocides, tragic accidents, and random natural disasters. There are powerful forces of evil at work against God's will, such as egotism, classism, racism, nationalism, militarism, and narcissism. The powers of greed, hate, and selfish ambition are strong in our world, infiltrating every human soul.

Does this adequately explain why God does not or cannot intervene to stop monstrous evil in the world? Not completely. The biblical writers offer no solutions, and the great thinkers—the theologians and philosophers—continue to debate issues of theodicy.

God, however, can and does utilize suffering in redemptive ways. In Paul's letter to the Romans, he calls attention to the process of redemptive growth that is achieved through suffering, declaring, "And not only that, but we also boast in our sufferings, knowing that suffering produces endurance, and endurance produces character, and character produces hope, and hope does not disappoint us, because God's love has been poured into our hearts through the Holy Spirit that has been given to us" (Rom 5:3–5). James, writing to disciples in exile, plagued by opposition, says, "My brothers and sisters, whenever you face trials of any kind, consider it nothing but joy, because you know that the testing of your faith produces endurance; and let endurance have its full effect, so that you may be mature and complete, lacking in nothing" (James 1:2–4).

The capacity to adopt a joyful response to suffering requires a perspective that sees suffering as an opportunity for spiritual development and growth. A college student sent the following letter to her parents,

> Dear Mom and Dad,
>
> I am sorry to be so long in writing. Unfortunately, all my stationery was burned up the night our dorm was set on fire by demonstrators. I am out of the hospital now and the doctors say my eyesight should return sooner or later. The wonderful boy, Bill, who rescued me from the fire kindly offered to share his little apartment with me until the dorm is rebuilt. He comes from a good family,

so you won't be surprised when I tell you that we are going to be married. In fact, Mom, since you always wanted a grandchild, you will be glad to know that next month you will be a grandparent.

P.S. Please disregard the above practice in English composition. There was no fire. I haven't been in the hospital. I'm not pregnant. And I don't have a steady boyfriend. But I did get a "D" in French and a "F" in chemistry, and I wanted to be sure you received this news in the proper perspective.

A perspective that enables us to see the big picture can enable us to nurture a positive outlook and attitude toward our trials and hardships.

Fr Richard Rohr contends that only great experiences of love and suffering "are strong enough to break down our usual ego defenses, crush our dual thinking, and open us up to the Mystery."[1] Rohr observes that *if we do not transform our pain, we are likely to transmit our pain to those around us*. Suffering can make us bitter and cause us to build walls that shut out God and other relationships, or it can soften our defenses and open us up to God's transforming grace. Rohr writes, "Struggling with one's own shadow self, facing interior conflicts and moral failures, undergoing rejection and abandonment, daily humiliations, experiencing any kind of abuse, or any form of limitation: all are gateways into deeper consciousness and the flowering of the soul."[2]

1. Rohr, *The Naked Now*, 122.
2. Ibid., 125.

This is no answer, however, to all questions of suffering. There are sufferings of such tragic proportions that it is difficult to find in them any redemptive value. Not long after the disastrous earthquake that devastated Haiti, one of the major television networks featured a piece on the humanitarian efforts of a seventy-eight year old doctor, who arrived in Haiti soon after the tragedy. He energetically dispensed what little medicines were available, mended broken bones, and offered assistance and comfort in any way he could. The news coverage highlighted a distraught boy, probably thirteen or fourteen years old, who lost his entire family. He was left with nothing and no one in the world, except his own life. He was so traumatized that he couldn't speak. The doctor indicated that the best treatment for the boy was to have someone stay with him at all times with whom he could make human contact. It is difficult to find any redemptive value in such pain.

For many people of faith it is enough to know that *God absorbs into God's self the world's anguish*. God participates in and is influenced by our misery and travail. The quintessential representation of this for disciples of Christ is the conviction that God became incarnate in Jesus of Nazareth, sharing the human plight and condition in a unique way. This reality is attested in Matthew's infancy narrative, "All this took place to fulfill what had been spoken by the Lord through the prophet: 'Look, the virgin shall conceive and bear a son, and they shall name him Emmanuel,' which means, 'God with us'" (Matt 1:22–23). God is with us, sharing our struggles and pain. God cannot stop tragedies from happening and people from dying, but God walks with us through all the common and uncommon experiences of life, especially times of great heartache and sorrow. *God is not a spectator in our suffering, but rather, an active participant in the ebb and flow of both the good and bad in our lives.* Our experience, rapturously joyful or horrendously painful, or anywhere in between, becomes part of God's experience.

In England during the Second World War some American soldiers were on furlough in London. They walked around the city in the aftermath of the German bombings and witnessed all the destruction. On Christmas day they happened to come upon a children's home. They were moved by the total absence of Christmas decorations and presents inside. The soldiers felt compassion for the children and reached into their pockets to give them whatever they had. One soldier went up to a little boy who reminded him of his nephew and asked him, "Son, what would you like for Christmas?" He said, "I just want somebody to love me." The mystery of "God with us" is a revelation of divine love. God says to each of us what Jesus heard God say at his baptism by John, "You are my beloved son, on you my favor rests."

The children in the preschool class had spent two afternoons making their parents a special ceramic Christmas surprise. The afternoon the children were to present it to their parents, one little boy, when he saw his parents coming to get him, became so excited that he ran toward them not watching where he was going. He ran right into another child and dropped his "surprise," which shattered into a hundred different pieces. The boy was as "shattered" as his surprise and began to cry. His father, thinking he was being helpful, went over and patted his son on the head, saying, "Shake it off son, it doesn't matter." His mother, on the other hand, after giving his father "that look," bent down, pulled him into her arms and said, "Oh, it does matter! It matters a great deal."

The miracle and mystery of "God with us" is God's way of conveying to humanity that we all matter, we matter a great deal. The Gospel of John declares in its opening prologue, "The Word became flesh and lived among us, and we have seen his glory . . . full of grace and truth" (John 1:14). *God stoops down, wraps her arms around us, and envelops us in divine love.*

When Jesus talks about the world he is very realistic. He speaks of wars and rumors of wars, nation rising up against nation and kingdom against kingdom, famines, earthquakes, and persecution of the faithful. There will even be times when "brother will betray brother to death, and a father his child, and children will rise against parents and have them put to death" (Matt 10:21). It's hard to imagine a more tragic plight than murderous hate rising up in one's own family. But even when the surface waters of our lives are churning in a fury, and we are tossed to and fro by the winds of hate and cruelty, deep down we can be sustained by a quiet joy. It's the joy of "God with us" and "God for us," affirming our true identity as the beloved children of God. I love the way Henry Nouwen describes this,

> People who have come to know the joy of God do not deny the darkness, but they choose not to live in it. They claim that the light that shines in the darkness can be trusted more than the darkness itself and that a little bit of light can dispel a lot of darkness. They point each other to flashes of light here and there, and remind each other

> that they reveal the hidden but real presence of God. They discover that there are people who heal each other's wounds, forgive each other's offenses, share their possessions, foster the spirit of community, celebrate the gifts they have received, and live in constant anticipation of the full manifestation of God's glory.[3]

Every day we must choose whether we will yield to the pain and pressures of life by being cynical, or whether we will overcome by nurturing a deeper joy.

Gerald Coffee was a captain in the U.S. Navy whose plane was downed over North Vietnam during our war with that country. He spent years as a POW confined to a small cell. In his book, *Beyond Survival*, he tells of the third Christmas he spent in prison. It was 1968 and he remembered it because it was the Christmas Eve the Vietnamese distributed some candy bars to the prisoners. The candy bars were wrapped in foil that was red on the outside and silver on the inside. Coffee flattened one wrapper and folded it into a swan. He turned a second wrapper into a rosette. He fashioned the third wrapper into a star. He thought of the star of Bethlehem.

He removed three straws from the broom in his cell and attached the paper ornaments to them. Then he jammed the straws into a crack in the wall above his bed. As he sat watching them in the light of the one yellow bulb that always shone in his cell, he thought about the simplicity of that first Christmas and what Christ's advent meant in his own life. It was his faith, he realized, that was sustaining him through his imprisonment. He writes, "Here

3. Nouwen, *The Return of the Prodigal Son*, 117.

there was nothing to distract me from the awesomeness of Christmas—no commercialism, no presents, little food. I was beginning to appreciate my own spirituality, because I had been stripped of everything by which I had measured my identity: rank, uniform, money, family. Yet I continued to find strength within. I realized that although I was hurting and lonely and scared, this might be the most significant Christmas of my life."[4]

How could that be? The "most significant Christmas" of his life? He was alone, stripped of everything, and unsure whether he would live or die. But they could not strip him of the one thing that mattered most: "God with us." What will it take for us to become attuned to the mystery and wonder of incarnation, of God with us, among us, in us, and for us?

Our world's version of joy is reflected in a line of a once-popular contemporary song, "Don't worry, be happy." The world dupes us into pursuing, buying, and consuming all sorts of things that we are told will bring us happiness. Maybe these things satisfy us for a while, but lives built on such flimsy materials all break down in the face of the evil of the Herods of our world and the unpredictable calamities that result in "wailing and loud lamentation." Rev Peter Gomes writes, "We are tempted to imagine Christmas as an 'out-of-body' experience, an antidote to the reality and brutality and crass materialism of a world that lost its way, but remember that the gospel begins with Caesar Augustus, in a real and fallen world."[5] It's a world of poverty and homelessness, of broken dreams and broken homes, a world

4. Quoted by Killinger, "Entertaining Mystery," 16.
5. Gomes, *Strength for the Journey*, 196.

where women are ravaged and children killed, a world of genocide and holocaust. But it is a world that God loves, a world Jesus gave his life for, a world where the Spirit is alive and well amid all the dirt, disease, and death. A world God refuses to give up on, and one in which God continues to work to redeem.

Author Ann Lamott and her two-year old son were staying in a condominium at Lake Tahoe. Because the area around Reno is such a hotbed for gambling, the rooms came equipped with curtains that blocked out every speck of light so one could sleep during the day. One afternoon she put her son to bed in his playpen in one of those pitch black rooms. He awoke, crawled out of his playpen and was at the door knocking. Somehow he managed to push the little button on the doorknob that locked it from the inside. He cried out to her, "Mommy, Mommy," but she couldn't open the door. She said to him, "Jiggle the door knob, darling." It soon became apparent to the little boy that he could not open the door and panic set in. He began sobbing. So his mother ran around like crazy, trying everything she could think of to get the door open. She called the rental agency where she left a message. She called the manager where she left another message. While she was running back and forth, trying to figure out what to do, there, in this pitch dark room was her terrified little child.

Finally, she did the only thing she could do, which was to slide her fingers underneath the door where there were a few centimeters of space. She kept telling him over and over to bend down and find her fingers. And somehow he did. So they stayed like that for a long time, connected on the floor, her son feeling her presence, feeling her warmth, feeling her love.[6]

Lamott's experience with her son reflects the essence of the good news that we celebrate at Christmas. *The love of God reaches out to us, even when we have locked the door from the inside.* Even when we have intentionally shut God out, because we loved the darkness more than the light, because we wanted to do our own thing, go our own way, and pursue our own selfish path. Even though the mess we are in is a mess we have made, God reaches out to us, like this mother connecting with her son or like the father in the story of the prodigal (Luke 15:11–24). God does not force God's self upon us or manipulate our freedom and our circumstances, but God reaches out to us, whispering our names, touching us in soft, simple, non-intrusive ways.

Can we trust that God is with us today, right now, whatever our condition and wherever we find ourselves? Jean Vanier says that persons with mental disabilities are excellent teachers when it comes to trust. In a society of aggressive competition they can teach us about what is important and how to live in the moment. They are not weighed down by the past, nor anxious toward the future. They live in the moment in a spirit of trust.

Vanier tells about the time one of their European communities went on a pilgrimage to Rome and had an audience with Pope John Paul II. While they were waiting for him to arrive, Fabio, a young man with mental disabilities, walked up and sat down in the Pope's chair. It was obviously the best seat in the room, which is why Fabio was attracted to it. The Bishops were not sure what to do. An assistant,

---

6. Referenced in Daniel, "The Preacher," 31.

however, helped Fabio find another chair. Fabio wasn't fearful about angering the Bishops or what the Pope might think or do. He was living in the moment from a place of inner freedom.[7] If we could find the courage to trust in the living presence of Christ—abiding in us, making his home with us, traveling with us as companion and partner on our daily pilgrimage—then we too, might discover the joy of being fully alive in the present moment, as we surrender our resentments over the past and our worries about the future.

An artist was painting a bleak picture of a winter storm sweeping across the countryside. Over in the corner was a cabin that looked dead and hopeless. But with one small stroke, the painter dramatically changed the mood of the picture. He took the tip of his brush, dipped it in gold paint, touched one window of the cabin, and the golden glow from that cabin transformed the picture from one of coldness and gloom to one of warmth and welcome.

No matter how dark the night or how fierce the storm, the warm glow of "God with us" shimmers in our hearts. And that is sufficient, that is enough to get us through. By faith we claim the reality Paul wrote about to the church in Rome, "that neither death, nor life, nor angels, nor rulers, nor things present, nor things to come, nor powers, nor height, nor depth, nor anything else in all creation, will be able to separate us from the love of God in Christ Jesus our Lord" (Rom 8:38–39).

---

7. Vanier, *Becoming Human*, 93.

Bibliography

Borg, Marcus. *The Heart of Christianity: Rediscovering a Life of Faith.* New York: HarperSanFrancisco, 2003.

Campolo, Tony. *Let Me Tell You a Story.* W. Publishing Group, 2000.

———. *The Kingdom of God Is a Party: God's Radical Plan for His Family.* Dallas: Word, 1990.

Cather, Willa. "The Burglar's Christmas." No pages. Online: http://www.shortstoryarchive.com/c/burglars_christmas.html.

Coffee, Gerald. "Beyond Survival." *Reader's Digest* (December, 1989). Quoted in John Killinger, "Enterntaining Mystery," *Pulpit Digest* (November/December, 1992) 13–16.

Craddock, Fred. *Craddock Stories.* Edited by Mike Graves and Richard F. Ward. St. Louis: Chalice, 2001.

———. *Luke.* Interpretation: A Bible Commentary for Teaching and Preaching. Louisville: John Knox, 1990.

Dark, David. *The Sacredness of Questioning Everything.* Grand Rapids: Zondervan, 2009.

Dunn, James D. G. *The First and Second Letters to Timothy and The Letter to Titus.* The New Interpreters Bible, Vol. XI. Nashville: Abingdon, 2000.

Gomes, Peter J. *Strength for the Journey: Biblical Wisdom for Daily Living.* New York: HarperSanFrancisco, 2003.

———. *The Scandalous Gospel of Jesus: What So Good About the Good News?* New York: HarperCollins, 2007.

Jordan, Clarence. *The Substance of Faith: And Other Cotton Patch Sermons.* Edited by Dallas Lee. Forward by Jimmy Carter. Eugene, OR: Cascade, 2005.

Kid, Sue Monk. *When the Heart Waits: Spiritual Direction for Life's Sacred Questions.* New York: HarperSanFrancisco, 1990.

Killinger, John. "Finding God in a Busy World." Preaching Today, Tape No. 132. PreachingToday.com and Christianity Today International, 2006.

Lamott, Ann. *Operating Instructions*. New York: Ballantine, 1994. Quoted in Lillian Daniel, "The Preacher," 31–35. *Journal for Preachers* (Vol. XXXIII, Num. 1, Advent 2009).

Larson, Bruce. *Luke*. The Communicator's Commentary. Waco, Texas: Word, 1983.

Lassen, William. "Peace," In the ABD 5:206–12.

L'Engle, Madeleine. "A Sky Full of Children." In *Watch for the Light: Readings for Advent and Christmas*, 78–81. Farmington, PA: Plough, 2001.

Manning, Brennan. "Shipwrecked at the Stable." In *Watch for the Light: Readings for Advent and Christmas*, 187–203. Farmington, PA: Plough, 2001.

Nouwen, Henry J. M. *The Genesee Diary: Report from a Trappist Monastery*. London: Darton, Longman, and Todd, 1995.

———. *The Return of the Prodigal Son: A Story of Homecoming*. New York: Doubleday, 1992.

Queen, Chuck. *The Good News According to Jesus: A New Kind of Christianity for a New Kind of Christian*. Macon, Georgia: Smyth & Helwys, 2009.

Rohr, Richard. *Hope Against Darkness: The Transforming Vision of Saint Francis in an Age of Anxiety*. Cincinnati: St. Anthony, 2001.

———. *The Good News According to Luke: Spiritual Reflections*. New York: Crossroad, 1997.

———. *The Naked Now: Learning to See as the Mystics See*. New York: Crossroad, 2009.

Rollins, Peter. *How (Not) to Speak of God*. Brewster, Mass.: Paraclete, 2006.

Smith, James Byron. *Rich Mullins: An Arrow Pointing to Heaven*. Forward by Brennan Manning. Nashville: Broadman and Holman, 2000.

Steindl-Rast, Brother David. *Gratefulness, the Heart of Prayer: An Approach to Life in Fullness*. New York: Paulist, 1984.

Thomas, Gary. *The Glorious Pursuit: Embracing the Virtues of Christ*. Colorado Springs: NavPress, 1998.

Underhill, Evelyn. *The Ways of the Spirit*. Edited, with intro. by Grace Adolphsen Brame. New York: Crossroad, 2000.

Vanier, Jean. *Becoming Human*. New York: Paulist, 1998.

———. *Encountering the Other*. New York: Paulist, 2005.

Wink, Walter. *Engaging the Powers: Discernment and Resistance in a World of Domination*. Minneapolis: Augsburg, 1992.

Yaconelli, Michael. *Messy Spirituality: God's Annoying Love for Imperfect People*. Grand Rapids: Zondervan, 2002.

www.ingramcontent.com/pod-product-compliance
Lightning Source LLC
Chambersburg PA
CBHW070504090426
42735CB00012B/2671